Mel Bay's
Deluxe Dobro Tune Book

By Stacy Phillips

Dobro® is a registered trademark belonging to
Original Musical Instrument Co., Inc.; used by permission.

A cassette tape of the music in this book is now available. The publisher strongly recommends the use of this cassette tape along with the text to insure accuracy of interpretation and ease in learning.

Contents

Introduction

This is a tune book for Dobroists who have learned the basic playing techniques and are looking for some new musical ideas. It updates and replaces two earlier Mel Bay publications, *Fiddle Tunes and Breakdowns for Dobro* (1981) and *Traditional Tunes for Contemporary Dobro* (1983). Several blues tunes have been added, while about ten of my less successful efforts from the original books have been eliminated due to space constrictions.

Most of the titles are derived from the fiddle traditions of America and the British Isles. All are arranged for six-string steel guitar and, with the few exceptions noted in the text, are in the current standard Dobro G tuning. Counting from the sixth (heaviest) string, the tuning should be: G-B-D-G-B-D, with the top three strings an octave above the lower three.

I have been careful to reflect a solid feel for the general melodies, especially in some of the lesser-known tunes. However, all are arranged to reflect a Dobro's characteristics and not to slavishly imitate the way a fiddle would play them. There is more here than just the skeletal music. All the numbers have been liberally garnished with a grab bag of succulent ornamentations, variations, harmonizations, syncopations, ruminations, and general hot licks tailored to raise the libido of even jaded Dobroists. Hopefully you will be sufficiently aroused to either adopt them whole, or to use them as starting points for your own ideas. Try fitting any of these licks that tickle your fancy into other tunes with similar chord progressions.

The tunes are not ordered according to degree of difficulty, and their technical demands vary widely. The music is not meant to be sight read. Some of the tablatures are quite difficult (at least at first), so take it slowly as you work them out. Start with just the notes and timing, and gradually add the accidentals (like slides, accents, and hammer-ons). Using the accompanying tape at this juncture can be a great help. Licks that give you trouble can be controlled if you have patience. Similar bar maneuvers appear in many tunes, so time spent in the domestication of boisterous riffs should decrease as you go through the selections.

The tunes are performed slowly on the cassette to ease interpreting the tablature. On the tapes for the original books, I played the tunes closer to their usual tempos. If you are interested in hearing those versions, they are still available if you write to me care of Mel Bay Publications, Inc., #4 Industrial Drive, Pacific, MO 63069-0066. On the current tape I usually play each section once and leave out the repeats.

When confronted with an unfamiliar tune, try strumming through the chords a few times to acclimate your musical ear to the harmonic background. It will make it easier to absorb the melody.

A few of the tunes that are not in the key of G sound best to me with an open-string, banjo-like approach, that is, a droning, overlapping broad side of notes. For these I use a capo. In these pieces the tablature numbers are counted from the fret on which the capo is placed, not from the beginning of the fretboard. So a "2" refers to playing a string 2 frets higher than the fret on which the capo is placed. Dobro capos can be hard to come by. I occasionally deal in such items, so feel free to contact me with questions.

Fast tunes in the key of D have been a source of anxiety for Dobroists. Capoing 7 frets up the neck allows you to play as if you were in the key of G, but shortening the neck so much gives the Dobro a tinny tone. The main advantage of playing in G is the availability of open strings. Since D, B, and

G are also common to the D scale (as well as the C scale), they can be used for hammer-ons, pull-offs, and pseudo-melodic banjo-style playing, just as in the key of G. If you conscientiously go through all the D tunes that follow, the key with two sharps will no longer cause any apprehension.

Occasionally I have recommended right-hand fingering. If you find other ways of hitting the same notes that are more comfortable, by all means use them. This is especially true of the hammer-ons and pull-offs, which ease the picking demands on your right hand, whereas picking each note separately can add clarity to your playing. Notations of these techniques have often been omitted except in places where their use may not be obvious or I feel that one choice sounds particularly pleasing. You should be able to discriminate the differences on the accompanying tape.

Usually I have not indicated whether the bar should be laid across all the strings or if only the tip of the bar should touch the indicated frets. Most of the time the choice is obvious, as the former can cause annoying dissonances. Other times, letting the previous notes persist results in pleasing resonances.

This book should introduce you to some striking melodies and interesting ways to play ones you already know. Feel free to change any arrangement around to suit yourself. Use them as exercises and etudes to develop your technique. Above all, enjoy the music.

Stacy Phillips
September 1991

Stacy Phillips (photo by Peter Schwimmer).

The Don Ho Show in the Polynesian Palace in Waikiki, Hawaii. Left to right: Tony Trischka, Don Ho (holding the microphone for Stacy Phillips), Stacy Phillips, Dede Wyland, Ken Kosek.

Music Notation and Tablature

Here is a bit of a road map to light your way through the labyrinth of mystic symbols known as music notation and tablature.

Do not play pairs of eighth notes as written! Instead of ♪ ♪ they should be played closer to the feel of ♪♪ . The latter is the way swing rhythm divides up a beat and the former is more classical sounding. When you get the tunes up to speed, the timing comes out a bit of each with a dash of ♪ ♪ thrown in. It is customary to avoid the excess notation and symbolize the timing as simple eighth notes.

As is customary for the guitar, tablature notes actually sound an octave lower than written. This is to avoid having to use other than the treble clef. Forgive the technicality.

In the tablature, frets are notated only when the bar changes position or a note is picked. So tie lines (indicating an extension of time duration of notes) appear only in the music notation, but slurs are used in both. (They use the same symbol but for different purposes.)

There are no metronome markings for exact tempos. Any recommendations I make are purposely subjective and on the vague side. These instrumentals sound fine at a wide range of speeds, and playing for your own enjoyment, at a square dance, or taking a solo during a fiddler's show-off piece all call for different approaches. Let your ear be your guide.

Most of the tunes are set in cut time (¢). This is used to reduce the need for writing sixteenth notes (which are relatively hard to count if you are not an accomplished reader) by doubling the time duration of all notes and rests. So notes that are ordinarily sixteenth are written as eighth, eighth notes become quarter notes, 1/128 notes become 1/64 notes, etc.

The following is a list of the symbols I use that might require some explanation:

⤴ means a slide of indeterminate length up to the indicated note, usually 1 or 2 frets' worth, sometimes less than a fret.

⤵ means an indeterminate slide down to the indicated note.

↗ means an indeterminate slide up after the note is picked.

↘ means an indeterminate slide down after the note is picked.

"H" placed between two notes indicates you should pick the first note and then hammer on with the bar on the 2nd indicated fret. For example, "$_0$ H $_2$" means pick the open string then hit the 2nd fret of the same string with the bar. One pick and two notes sounded.

"P" placed between two notes indicates you should pick the first note with your right hand and then pull off the string with your bar to get the sound of the second note. For example, "$_1$ P $_0$" means pick the 1st fret of the indicated string and then pull the bar off to hear the open string. One pick and two notes sounded.

"T" indicates the thumb of your picking hand.

"I" indicates the index finger of your picking hand.

"M" indicates the middle finger of your picking hand.

These last three symbols appear under the tablature:

$\bar{\wedge}$ The legato symbol above a note in the tab means there should be no interruption of sound between the indicated note and the next, i.e., keep the bar on the strings. I usually use it to indicate a slide with both notes picked.

⌢ means to slide to all the notes enclosed by the slur sign. This is the same symbol as time extension of a note. I usually use it to indicate a slide with only the first note picked.

⦚ means a quick, dampened strum on the indicated fret.

"tr" means a trill. Slide quickly back and forth between the indicated notes.

( ) The parentheses mean a ghost note, i.e., a note at least partially dampened. I also use it to indicate a chord that is voluntary.

↑ placed to the right of a note means you should "choke" (i.e., pull) the indicated string with one or more of your dampening fingers of your bar hand so that its pitch is raised a half step (i.e., 1 fret). So "5 ↑" means that, even though the bar is on the 5th fret, the string is raised in pitch to the sound of the 6th fret.

↑↑ placed to the right of a note means you should choke it a whole step (i.e., 2 frets' worth). So "5 ↑↑" means that the bar is on the 5th fret and the note sounds as if it were on the 7th.

* placed to the right of a note means that the note is choked in pitch *up to* the indicated fret. This symbol occurs only with slanted bar positions. So

means that the bar is touching the second string midway between the 4th and 5th frets, and this string is choked until the second string sound the pitch of the 5th fret.

𝄉 A grace note is held for the shortest possible time.

⌇ means a wide, fast vibrato giving the note a slightly hysterical sound.

Facing page -
Stacy Phillips visits the Archduke of the Dobro
— Photo by Georgia Sheron
— Drawing by Todd Smith

Cindy

You might try playing the introduction of "Cindy" without hammering on, that is, by fingering it T-I-T-I-T.

In the second part, accenting the indicated notes will give a bouncy feel with a bluegrass rhythm backup. It also serves to give a bit of a melody line to this series of rolls. I hit all the accented notes with my thumb.

Carroll County Blues

"Carroll County"'s blues feel makes it a natural for Dobro. It exhibits some of the vagaries of old-time music, especially in the tacking on of a couple of extra measures in the first part.

The accents are important to get the right feel here. Then the second part meanders about like an undeveloped theme for as long as you would like before it heads back to the beginning. This part has no particular melody, so mix in your own brand of repetitive blues licks.

Play "Carroll County Blues" bouncy and medium slow. There is just one kickoff note (B♭) and a 2-measure tag.

9

Cowboy Waltz

I learned "Cowboy Waltz" from one of the first New Lost City Ramblers records and have not heard it on record since. Lots of indeterminate slides give the wailing effect of old-timey fiddle and serve to accent the notes to which you slide. You might be amused by the pedal-point lick over the E7-to-A7 change.

Paddywack

Here is a straight-ahead jig I learned from banjo guru Tony Trischka. I figure, if it sounds good on a five-string, how much more so on a Dobro. As with all the tablatures in this book, the barring shown is just suggested, and you might like to do it another way. For example, an alternate 2nd measure is shown after the main body of the tune.

The fingering for the first 2 measures is: T-I-M-I-M-I   T-I-T-I-T-I

I hit the last note of the 5th measure open (instead of 7th fret, third string) to allow me to move the bar to the next note without sliding. In the 9th and 14th measures, I play the same C and D notes with different fingerings because the preceding notes put the bar on different frets.

Alternate second
measure fretting

11

Kitchen Girl

"Kitchen Girl" switches from A to A minor, so watch the key-signature change in the middle.
Try to play the E-F♯-E notes in the 2nd measure without any slide.

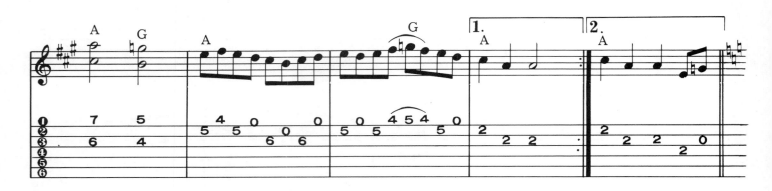

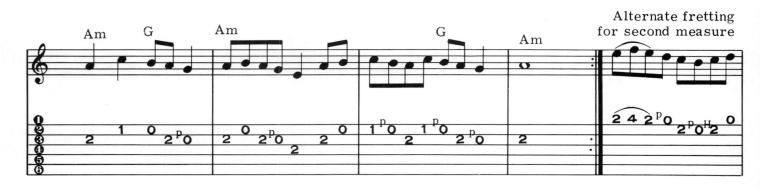

Turkey in the Straw

The suggested fingering for the kickoff and first 2 measures of "Turkey in the Straw" is:

  I-T   P-T-I-H-P-I-T-H   I-P-H-I-I-T-H

In the 4th measure of the second part, I use a crossover fingering, i.e., the index finger on a higher string than the middle: I-T-I-M-I-T.

In the 5th measure of the second part, you might play a "ghost strum" to emphasize the first note. To do this, tilt the bar so it touches only the first string on the 5th fret, but leave the pinky and ring finger of your left hand on all the strings. Strum quickly with your right thumb. The lower five strings are muted (hence "ghost") by the left hand but still give a percussive sound. At the end of this old chestnut, I have given a suitably moss-covered tag.

Saint Anne's Reel

"Saint Anne's Reel" comes out of the British tradition by way of bleak New England winters. The F♯-G-F♯ slides in the 1st and 5th measures must be played quickly and accurately. If they are fretted hesitantly, the whole piece will sound flimsy. This tune is meant to be played up tempo. The last 2 measures are a tag module that can be tacked onto most any key-of-D tune.

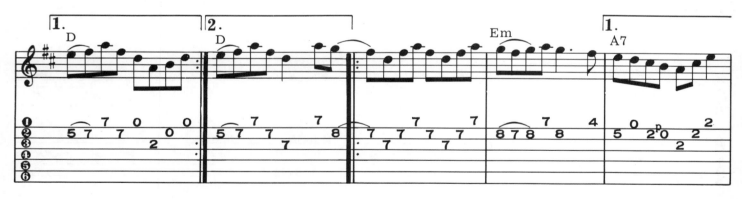

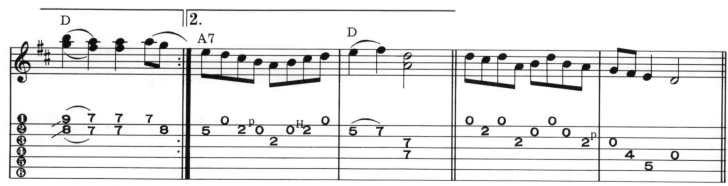

Jennifer Waltz

"Jennifer Waltz" is based on the playing of the founder of bluegrass Dobro, Buck Graves. He manages to infuse even a somewhat shmaltzy tune like this with some blues. It is one of his great talents to make simple riffs interesting. The indicated slides are broad with some vibrato. The first B note is fretted instead of being picked on the open second string to enable vibrato. A slightly fancier setting of the first 2 measures follows the main body of the tune.

Resonator guitars built by Bobby Wolfe, Route 1, Box 815D, Davidson, NC 28036.

Cherokee Shuffle

I learned "Cherokee Shuffle" from mandolinist-Dobroist Artie Rose. Its structure is reminiscent of another fiddle tune, "Lost Indian," but with a second section added on. This tune is in the key of A but is easiest on Dobro when played in open position, so I have arranged it for a capo on the 2nd fret. The numbers in the tablature refer to the number of frets from the capo that the bar must be placed. So the first note of this piece is played on the open fourth string and, since there is a capo on the 2nd fret, that note sounds 2 frets higher than without a capo (i.e., an E instead of a D).

Alternate 1st 4 measures

Bill Cheatham

"Bill Cheatham," sometimes called "Bill Cheatum," "Bill Cheat 'Em," or "Sluggo Cheatham," is capoed on the 2nd fret for this arrangement. John Burke, fiddle-tune maven of both coasts, tells me this tune is named for Cheatham County, Tennessee, which is as likely an explanation as any. It begins with a Dobro variation of the classic fiddle kickoff, and the tag is a variation of the one used in "Turkey in the Straw." The recommended fingering for the 3rd measure of the melody (the D chord) is T-I-T-I-M-T-I.

18

Sally Ann

"Sally Ann" is set in Texas style, and I think that the minor chords add some beauty to the melody. Do the second part an extra two times before returning to the first section.

As an added bonus, there is a double tag on the end. The first half is similar to the one in "Turkey in the Straw," and the second is in neo-primitive style. The first four notes in the 2nd measure of the tag might be fretted as I-T-I-T.

Folding Down the Sheets

"Folding Down the Sheets" is another British tune I learned from Tony Trischka, and it is not meant to be played at breakdown speeds. The 1st measure of the second part presents particular technique problems if you want to play it without slides. Use just the thumb and index finger to pick it, and damp quickly after each note with the trailing fingers of your left hand.

Back Up and Push

"Back Up and Push," sometimes suggestively titled "Rubber Dolly," is a good-natured tune usually done at breakneck tempos. The first section is somewhat in the style of Shot Jackson, purveyor of Shobro resonator guitars. The lick in the 6th measure is a good exercise to improve the accuracy of your slanted bar positions. Practice the slide up and down from the 15th to the 17th frets slowly at first, always making sure of your in-tuneness. Eventually, your left hand will memorize this move.

The second section has no particular melody, so I have tossed in a few random licks for your picking pleasure. In the first 2 measures, keep the bar on the bottom five strings of the 10th fret so the notes overlap. In the 2nd measure, have the second string choked before picking it so there is no glissando effect. Start choking it towards the end of the previous measure.

John's Lover Is Gone

While I was hanging out at the Puget Sound Guitar Workshop, I learned this tune from a fine northwestern old-time fiddler, Jack Link. The name is either "John's Lover Is Gone" or his liver, it was never made quite clear to me. It is a member of the "hell-bent for leather" (or liver) tunes in southeastern style and can be played with wild abandon. The second verse is pretty much like the first, only an octave lower. Those of you attuned to the machinations of old-time fiddlers will recognize this as a common ploy.

Prisoner's Song

In the "Prisoner's Song" the first 8 measures are pretty close to the melody, then, in the time-honored traditions of bluegrass, I have varied the melodic and then rhythmic structures of the tune in the next 8.

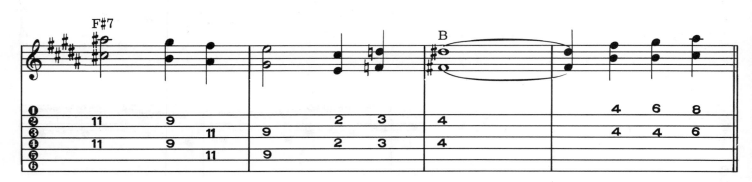

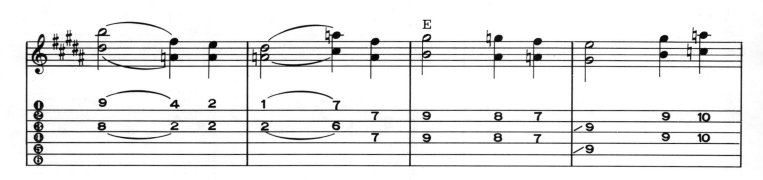

John Hardy

     "John Hardy" is arranged for breakdown speeds and is noteworthy for a few of the bluegrass clichés I have sprinkled through it. The introductory walk-up is the standard for fast tunes, while the tag is an Earl Scruggs banjo-style ending. Other yawn-inducing standard licks can be found in measures 5, 10, and 17 through 20. The latter is a paraphrasing of a particularly insidious banjo riff. The 10th and 18th measures should start out in slant positions.

Colored Aristocracy

I learned the catchy "Colored Aristocracy" from the New Lost City Ramblers. This stately tune should not be played at breakdown tempo.

Paul Beard resophonic guitars (14118 Marsh Pike, Hagerstown, MD 21742). Right: Six-string mahogany body. Below: Eight-string mahogany body. Paul also offers a fine video on resophonic guitar set-up and maintenance.

Bully of the Town

In a typical bluegrass style, "Bully of the Town" has a first part filled with fast notes, while the second part has more half and whole notes, legato slides, and double stops. Compare this to a tune like Bill Monroe's "Panhandle Country," in which the first part has the double stops and the second has the fast series of notes. This is also true, to an extent, of "Back Up and Push." The first couple of measures are a paraphrasing of the banjo kickoffs to "Foggy Mountain Breakdown" and "Bluegrass Breakdown" and fit right into the tune's structure. The G-diminished chord in the 2nd measure is strictly voluntary (hence the parentheses), but it adds harmonic movement. In the 7th measure, keep the bar on the strings so that the 2nd four notes are played with a forward slant on the third and fifth strings.

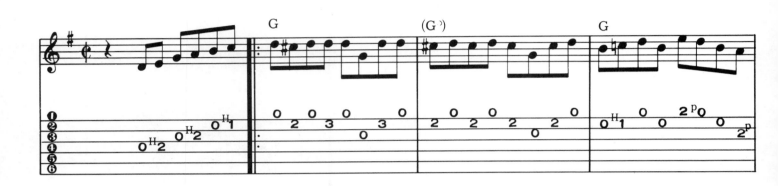

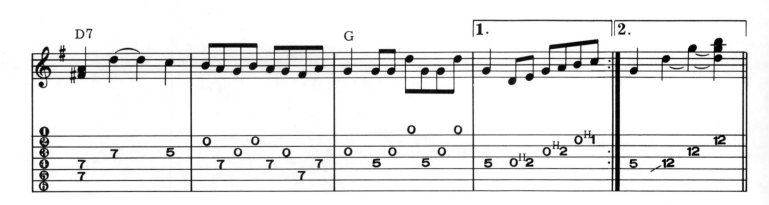

28

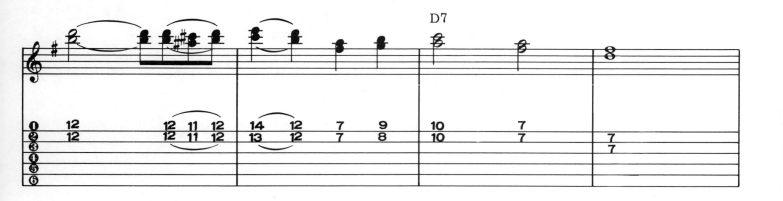

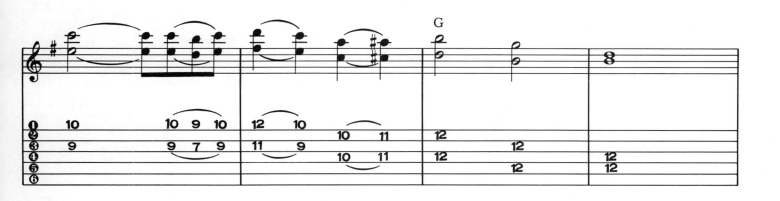

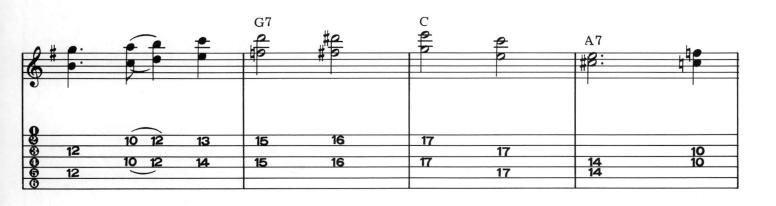

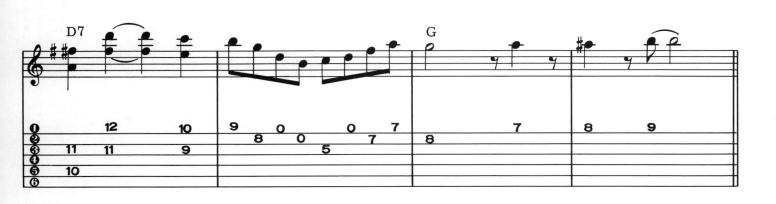

Napoleon Crossing the Rhine

"Napoleon Crossing the Rhine" is another stately British Isles-sounding air meant to be played at an unrushed tempo. The six-note figure that begins on an E that appears at the end of the 2nd measure and continues into the 3rd is a very handy lick and worth some practice to get it cleanly. Keep the two damping fingers of your barring hand (ring and pinky) anchored, and use the tip of the bar to play the riff. You might prefer to fret the C and A notes in the 3rd measure on the 10th fret, fourth and fifth strings respectively.

The 2nd measure of the second part might use this fingering: M-I-T-I-M-T-I. On the fourth note, the index finger crosses under the thumb to pick a lower string, a tricky but useful maneuver.

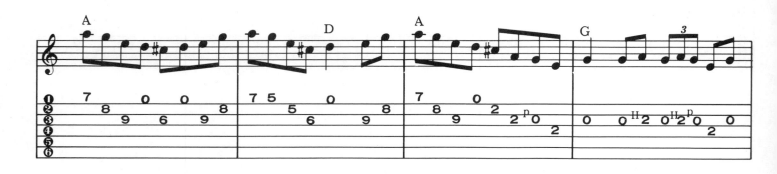

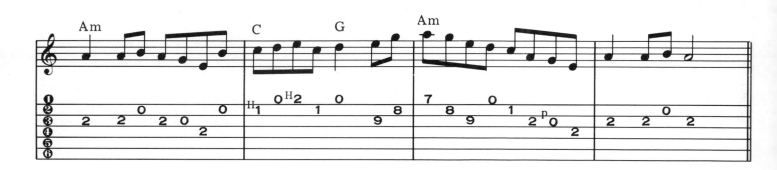

Liberty Dance

"Liberty Dance" shows how choking the strings can avoid a lot of bar movement and, in the long run, enable you to play at faster tempos. In the kickoff and 4th measure, choking the second string lets you keep the bar on the 7th fret instead of shifting back and forth between the 7th and 8th. You might wish to do similar choking in the 6th measure instead of the suggested fretting. The last D note in the 1st measure is played on an open string to ease moving the bar to the 4th fret to begin the next measure.

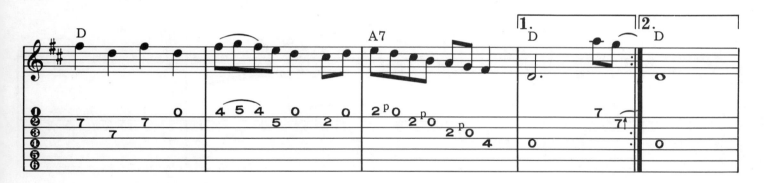

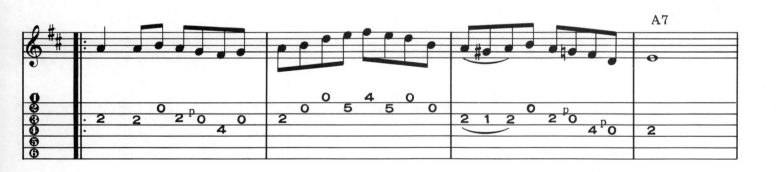

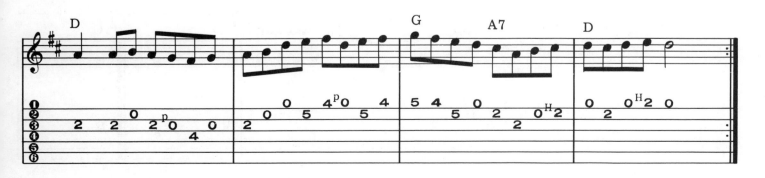

Whistling Rufus

"Whistling Rufus" utilizes choking in the same manner as "Liberty Dance." The 4th measure features a lick of satisfying contrary motion that you might wish to stockpile for future use.

To imitate a whistling sound, some fiddlers play the second section very close to the bridge, which emphasizes the higher harmonics of the strings. With that in mind, this part is arranged for the use of that most ephemeral of Dobro sounds, artificial harmonics (a.h.). Use vibrato to help the sustained notes to keep sounding. The last 3 measures do not use harmonics.

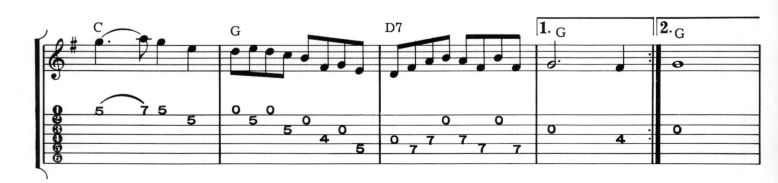

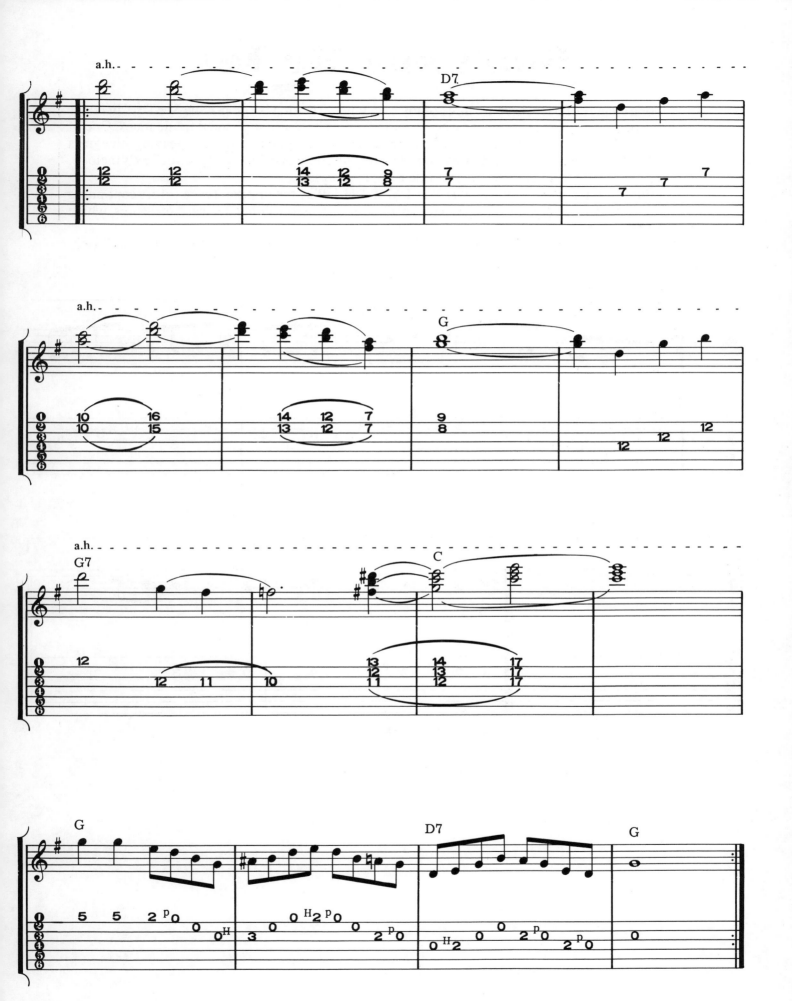

Don't Sue Me Tex

For a change of pace, here are three of my own tunes. The first is "Don't Sue Me Tex" in honor of Tex Logan, an electrical engineer who plays and writes hard-driving modal fiddle tunes. One of them, called "Get Along Jody," marked the reticence his daughter showed in leaving bluegrass festivals. I had not heard it for many years when I wrote this based on dim memories of Tex's melody. It came out close enough for the present title to be appropriate.

I finger the 1st measure as follows: T-H-I-M-T-I-H-I. Play the first part twice before continuing with the second. You might want to then replay the first part before doing the last 2 measures, which are another all-purpose ending.

Tony Trischka's band, Skyline, recorded this on their first Flying Fish album, *Late to Work*.

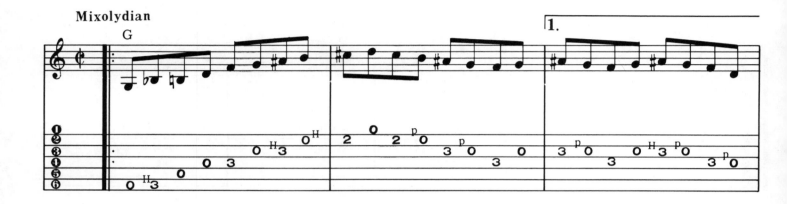

© Stacy Phillips 1980

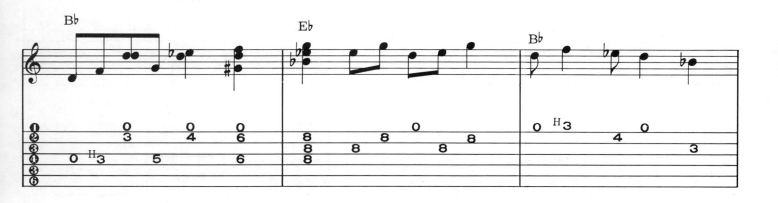

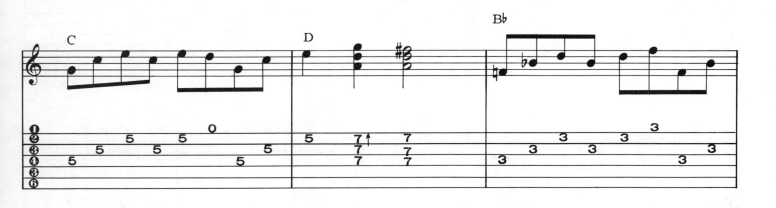

Old Turnpike Two-Step

The first 2 measures of "Old Turnpike Two-Step" are a lick that I use occasionally as part of my warm-up exercises. To make it more interesting, I decided to write a tune around it. The first part of both verses can help educate your fingers to hit different strings accurately. In the second verse, the picking pattern in the first 2 measures is sort of the reverse of the first verse. The second half of the second verse is a good exercise in slanting the bar and choking the string.

1st verse

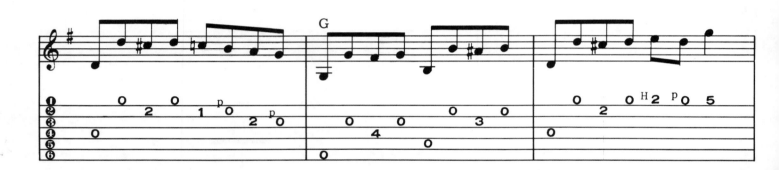

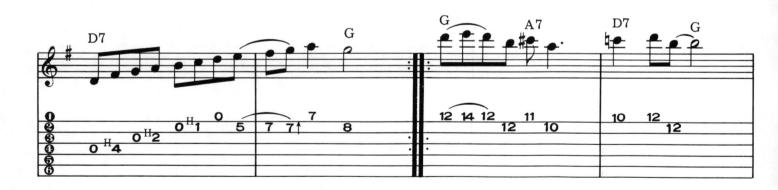

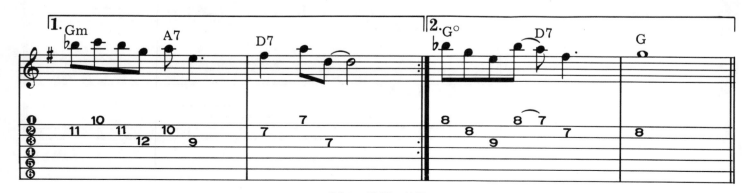

2nd verse

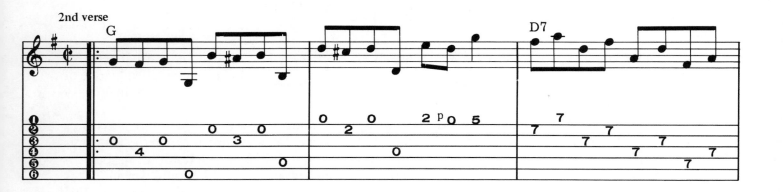

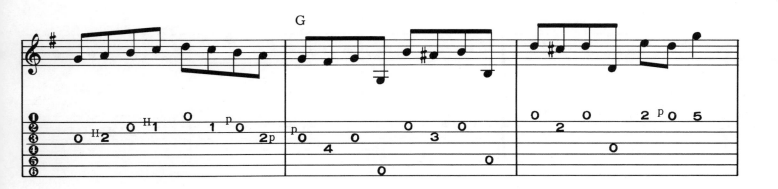

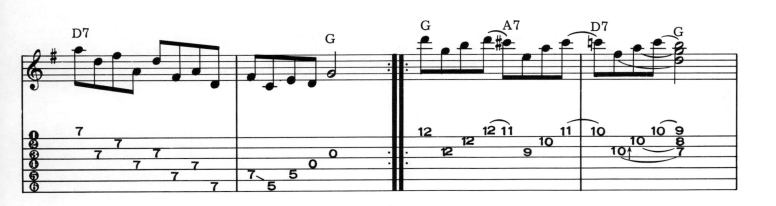

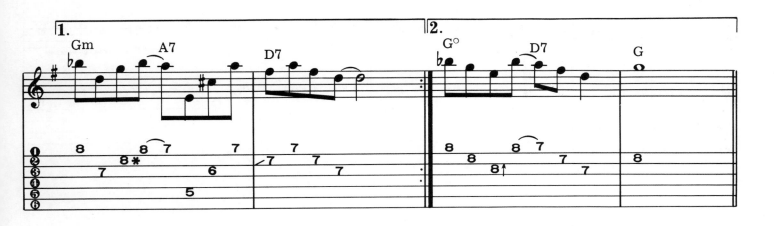

37

Wild Cargo

I used to live upstairs from the Wild Cargo Pet Shoppe, which specialized in unusual pets like coati mundi and boa constrictors. Each morning I expected to awaken to being eyeballed by one of the store's more exotic denizens. I have tried to transfer this unsettling experience to the queasy progressions of this tune.

"Wild Cargo" uses modal tuning to ease playing in G minor. This way you do not have to worry about the B♮ string, which does not fit into the G-minor scale. Do not damp through the measures of E♭ minor, so when you release the choke on the fourth string, 15th fret, it will reinforce the octave-higher first string, 15th fret, at the end of the measure. The heavy gauge of the fourth string makes choking difficult, so if your choking finger hurts, stop for a while. Do not strain your muscles. This second part shows some of the nice three-string chords you can get with modal tuning.

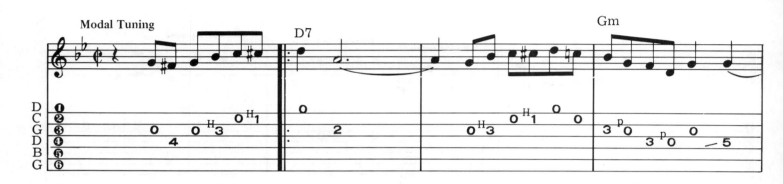

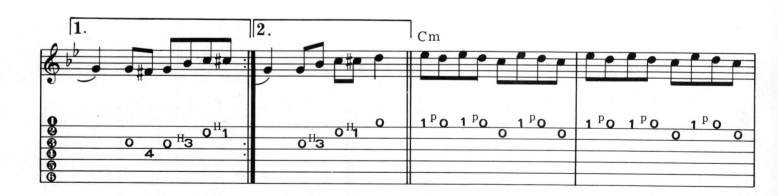

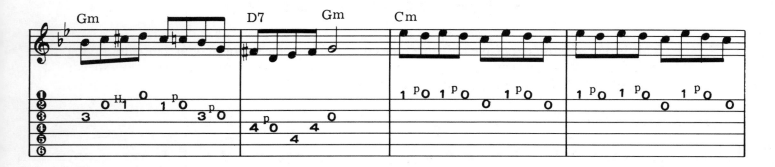

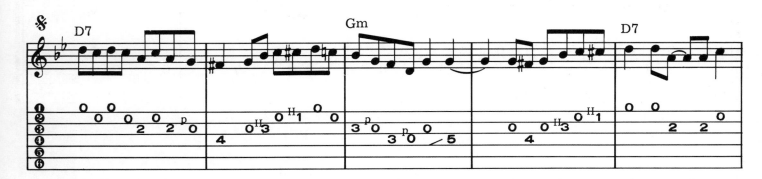

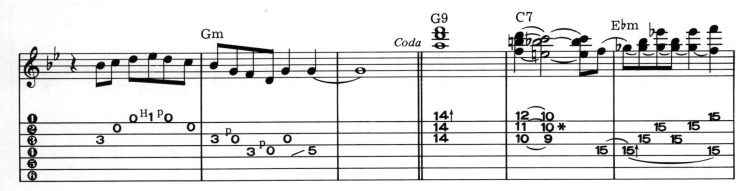

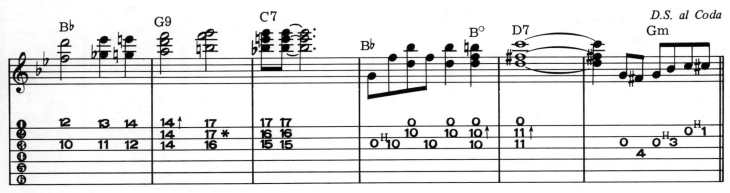

39

Old Joe Clark

This is one of those pervasive old-time tunes that you can get sick of playing but, after giving it an extended vacation, you can once again discover its joys. It will take some practice at slow speeds to do the pulls in the 1st measure cleanly and in rhythm.

capo on second fret

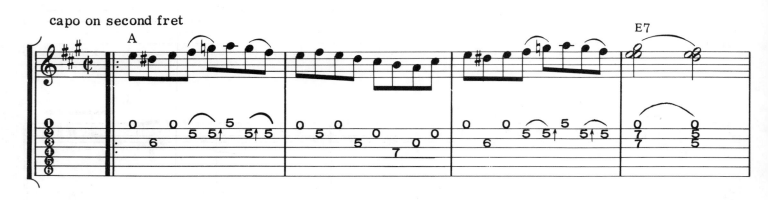

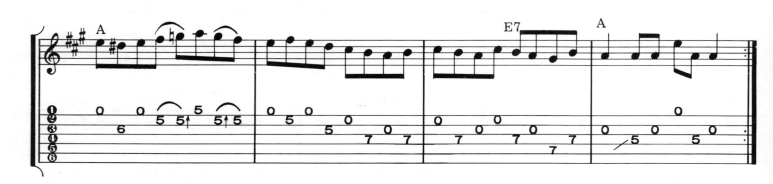

Resonator guitars built by Tim Scheerhorn (5636 Bentbrook, Kentwood, MI 49508). He uses a new system of metal baffles instead of wooden sound wells.

Homecoming Waltz

"Homecoming Waltz" is a three-part Texas tune that I have arranged as an exercise in alternate-string double stops with plenty of slant positions. Vibrato is an absolute must on this piece. The first three double stops are another version of a walk-up that I have used a few times previously. Watch for the reverse slants sprinkled through this tablature. The whole first part can be played without lifting the bar off of the strings. The third part goes to the key of D. Then repeat the first two parts and end back in the key of A.

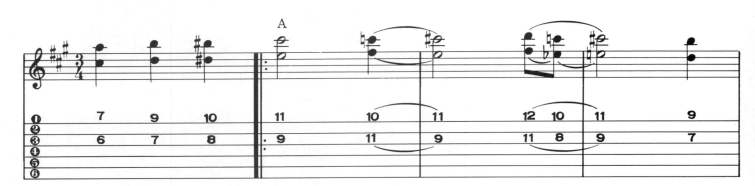

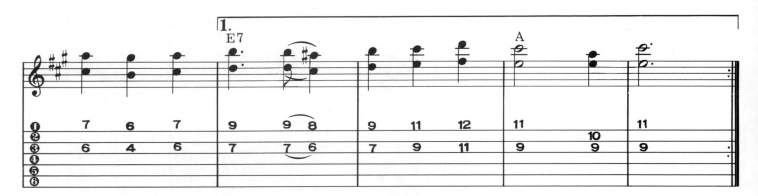

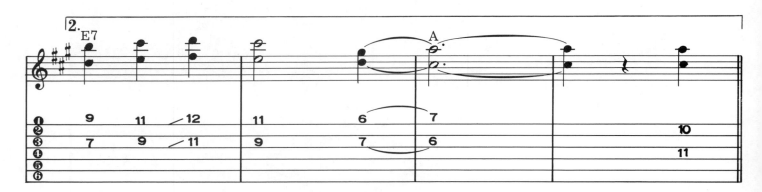

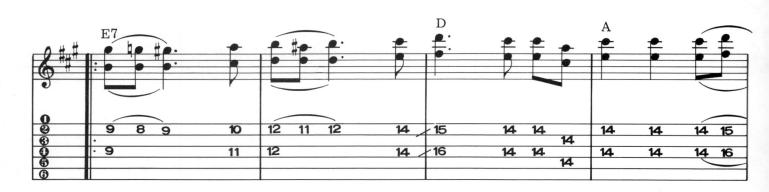

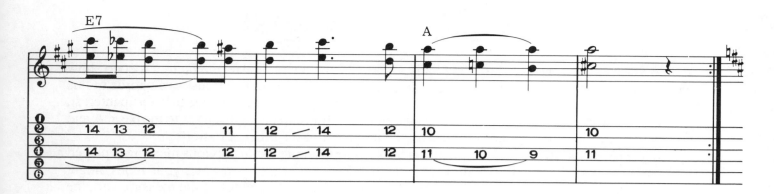

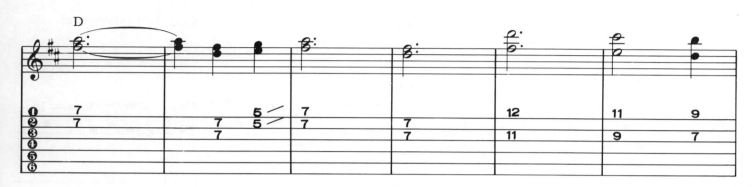

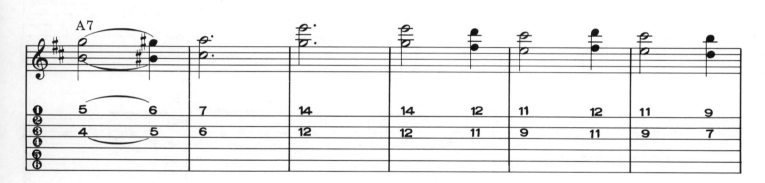

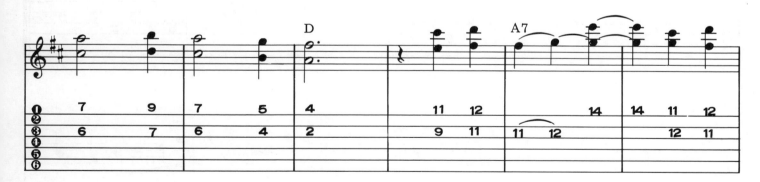

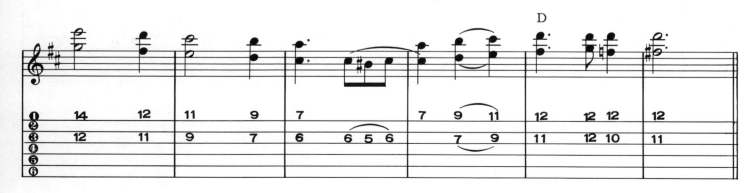

Sally Goodin

Wild-eyed fiddlers have built up "Sally Goodin" from a simple dance tune to a rococo show piece, and here are ten variations in the Texas manner. There are basically just two chords in this number but Texas guitarists, being a breed apart, tend to throw in some extra ones to keep up interest. I have given an example of some of them on the first variation and then gone back to the basic A and E7 afterwards. These fancy chords will work behind most of the other variations.

In the second section, the 3rd measure is tricky. The last note of the previous measure is played with the thumb so the picking continues: I-M-I-T-I-M-I-T. On the third note, your index finger crosses over the middle one to pick a higher string. Play the last five notes of the measure with the tip of the bar, not as a slant position.

The last variation features some natural harmonics. After this section, repeat the first one and proceed to the 4-measure tag.

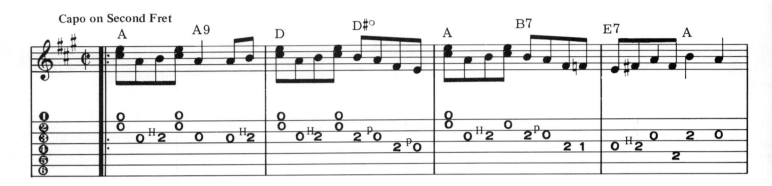

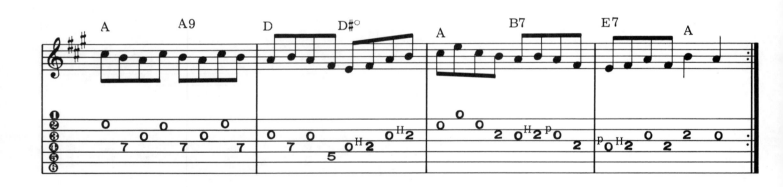

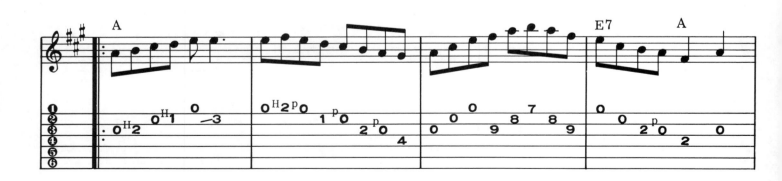

44

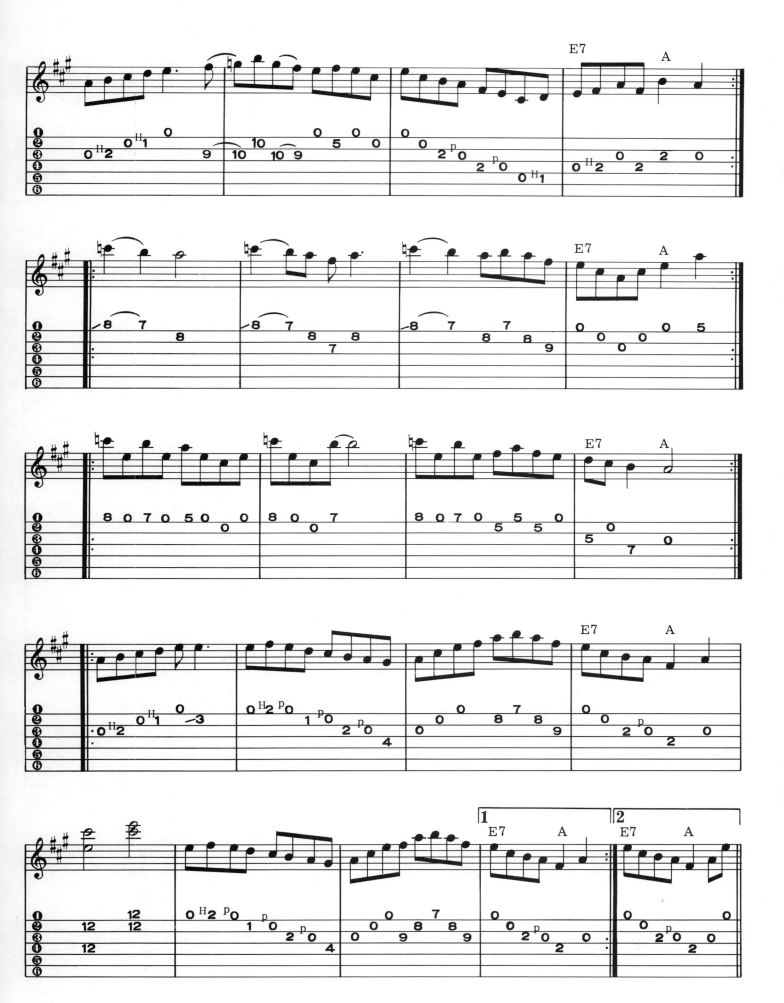

Pacific Slope Reel

I picked up "Pacific Slope Reel" from fiddler and raconteur Ken Kosek. He can be heard playing on many a cat-food and deodorant commercial, but his visage is rarely spotted outside the seamy environs of New York City. The melody certainly evokes a longing for the open spaces of the Slope (California, Washington, Oregon, Utah, and Nevada).

Obey the accent sign in the 1st measure and you will be rewarded with a distinctly bouncy sensation. On the accompanying cassette, it is tricky to pick up the beat because of this syncopation. Count along and follow the music. All will be illuminated.

Wait to choke the second string until the downbeat of the 2nd measure, and then do so quickly to minimize the slide effect.

Mr. Kosek's latest recorded effort can be heard on the Rounder record *Hasty Lonesome*. Try it.

Capo on second fret

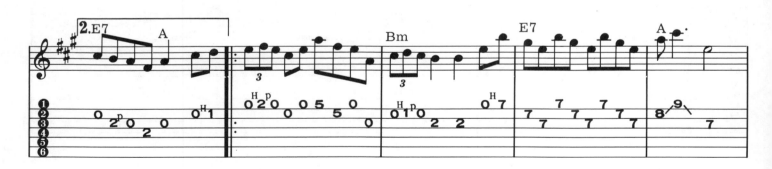

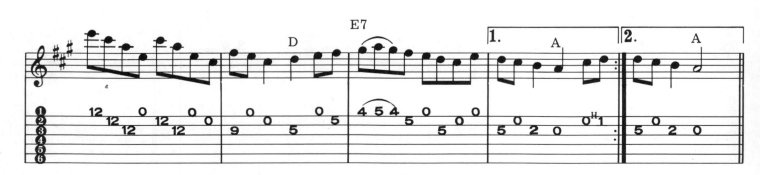

Breakfast Special at its first rehearsal. Left to right: Stacy Phillips, Roger Mason, Anthony Trischka, James Tolles, Kenneth Kosek, and Andrew Statman (photo by Jim McGuire).

Golden Slippers

No doubt you have heard any number of tired double-fiddle arrangements of "Golden Slippers." This worn-down war horse is in dire need of a Dobro to spruce it up. Play it at the "cruising speed" marker on your metronome.

Try some of the indicated hammer-ons and pull-offs with separate picking. If the triplets go by too quickly, you can play the triplet's first note as a quarter note and leave out the other two.

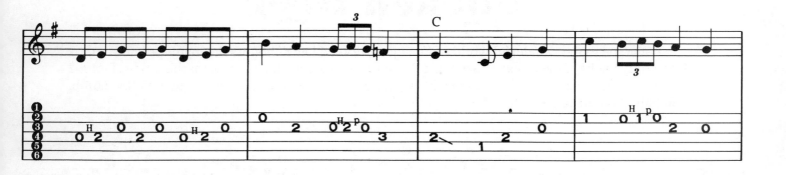
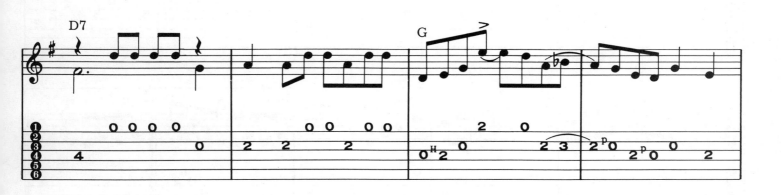
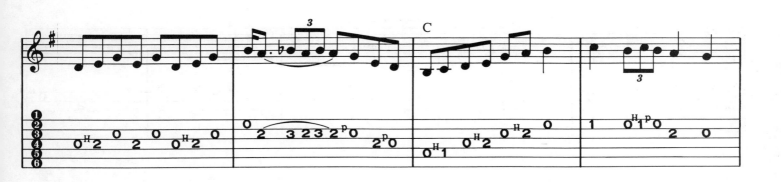
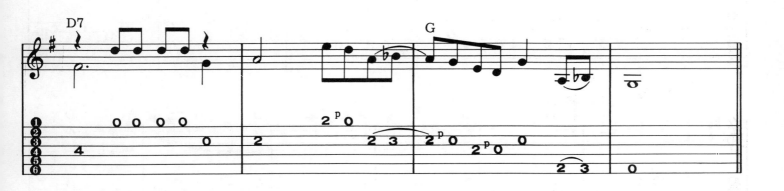

Forked Deer

Welcome to the wonderful world of D major. "Forked Deer" honors the many-pointed antlers of the randy bucks of the forest. What could be a more appropriate tune for the rambunctious Dobro?

In the 10th measure of the second edition, there is a dampened, upward scrape with the thumb, anticipating the next measure's A note on the downbeat.

Sailor's Hornpipe

When you arrange one of these tunes to your own liking, one of the things to consider is whether to lay the bar across all strings (to ease overlapping of notes) or to use the tip to touch one string only. For example, on the tape of "Sailor's Hornpipe," I use the tip of the bar up to the third note of the 2nd measure, and then quickly lay the bar flat for the 2nd fret, third and second strings. Then it is back to the tip for the open first string onward, until a similar move in the 7th measure, 2nd fret, fifth and fourth strings. Once again it's back to the dainty use of the tip of the bar until the second section, where all of measures 1 and 3 demand the esthetic use of the whole bar.

Be aware of what pedal-steel guitarists call "bar chatter." When you quickly place the bar flat, make sure that the trailing fingers of your left hand land first to minimize any incidental bar rattles.

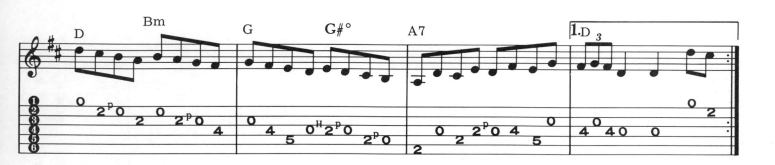

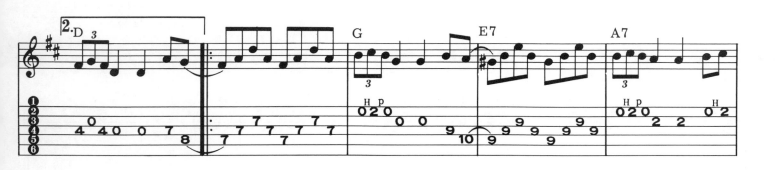

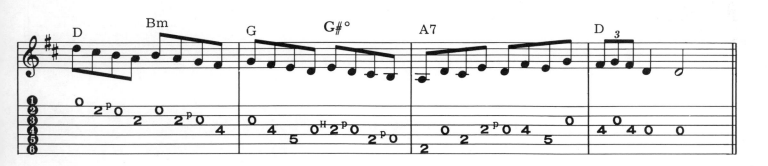

Put Your Little Foot

"Put Your Little Foot" harkens to the days of the minuet. On slow ones, you can concentrate on a mellow vibrato and the difference between slides with picking (horizontal lines in the tablature, starting with the 1st measure) and without picking (slur lines in the 5th measure of the second part). I have indicated the difference in a few tunes and left the rest to your discretion.

When the horizontal line is followed by a diagonal one, as at the end of the 3rd and 9th measures, the slide starts immediately upon picking and is prolonged just enough to arrive at the next note at the right moment. The horizontal line only indicates holding the picked note for its full duration and then executing a quick slide to the next indicated fret. When the next notes are on the same fret (e.g., the 4th measure), let the notes overlap.

Enough subtleties. It is easier to hear than describe.

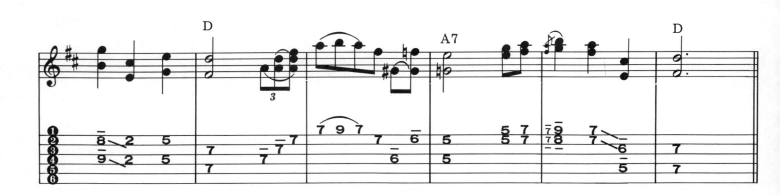

Mike Auldridge (photo by Jim McGuire).

Big John McNeil

Mr. McNeil's tune is acceptable from square-dance tempos to tachyon speeds. It comes from Scotland by way of Canada (eh), and the first section is similar to the American "Durham's Bull." The 7th and 8th measures are particularly demanding. Capo up 2 frets and let 'er rip.

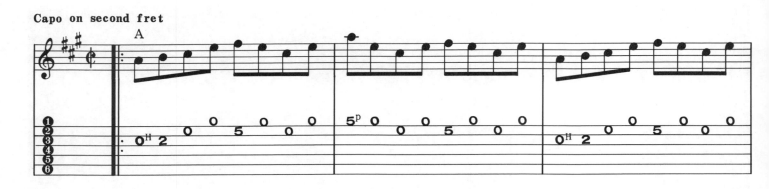

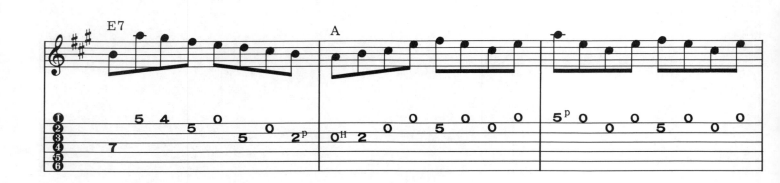

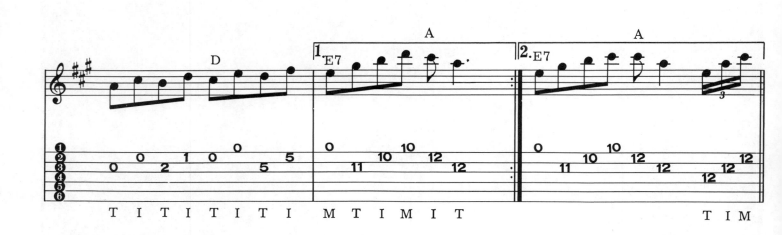

54

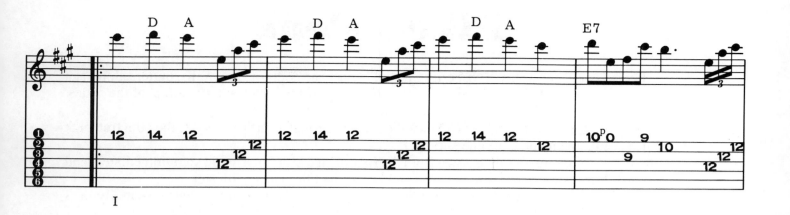

I

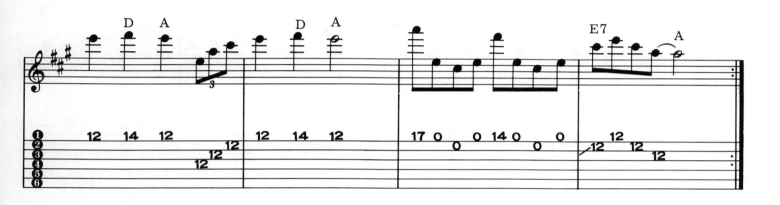

Alternate second section

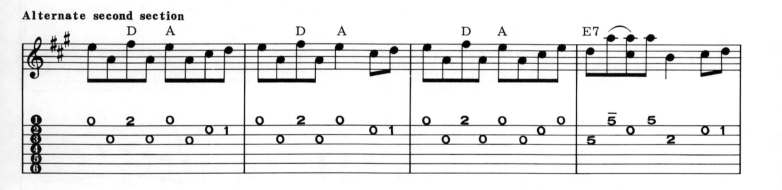

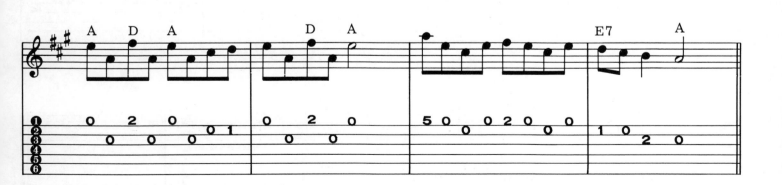

Pike's Peak

"Pike's Peak," known as "Prosperity Special" under the aegis of Bob Wills, putters along at a swingy tempo. I have indicated a couple of legato notes that are important to the feel of the slides, but there are other candidates for this effect which I will leave to your imagination.

In the 11th measure, as soon as you pick the second through fourth strings on the 10th fret, pick the fourth string again and continue sliding.

In the 13th measure, the slide down from the first string, 12th fret, should start immediately and reach the 10th fret simultaneously with the picking of the third string, 9th fret.

The double stop in parentheses goes by so quickly at the usual tempo that, essentially, it is "ghosted" but not dampened. The F-to-A7 chord progression is in the Wills style.

Growling Old Man and Growling Old Woman

The first section of this Canadian-sounding tune is supposed to represent the gruff old codger, while the second goes into the higher register for the shrill harridan.

Watch out for the 8th measure. Try to hit all the notes with the tip of the bar. A busier first section and simpler last 2 measures are appended.

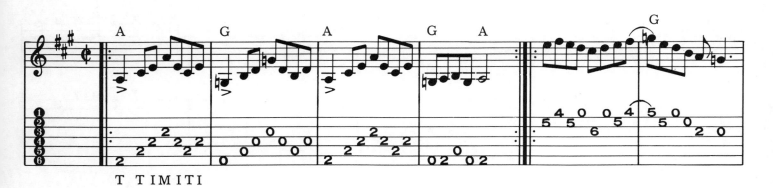

T T I M I T I

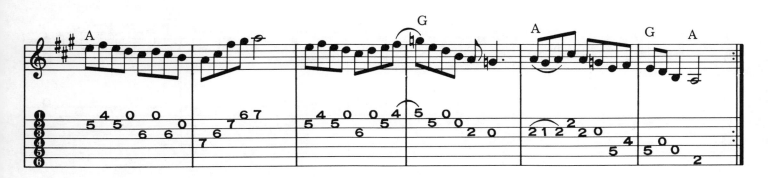

Alternate first section

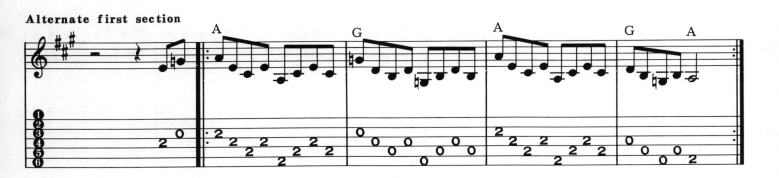

Alternate last two measures

Rickett's Hornpipe

In the Old Country, hornpipes are generally played with a choppy 𝄒 rhythm. In the New World this has been smoothed out towards ♫ but between the two. Do not play it as 𝄒. This comes out rather lifeless (in a rhythmic sense) and too "classical" sounding.

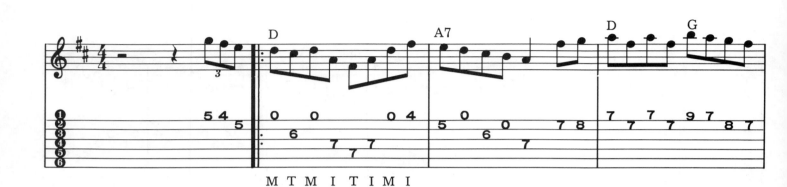

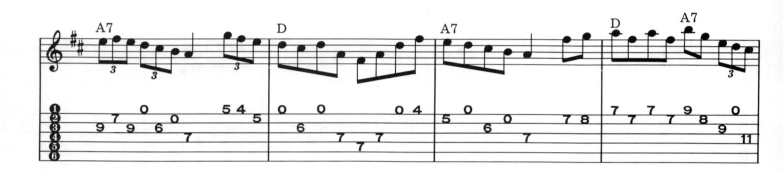

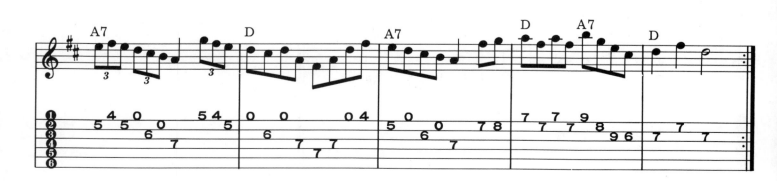

British Field Marshal
at New Orleans

I discovered "British Field Marshal" on an undeservedly obscure album of the Deseret String Band. Does it really go back to the 8th of January, 1812? A field marshal is the highest ranking officer, above general. Edward Pakenham was the head of British forces at the Battle of New Orleans. He signalled the charge before preparations were complete and died trying to rally his men. The decisive fight lasted five minutes.

Play this at a loping, medium tempo. There is a bit of a march feel to it. Except for the 7th measure, try to play all the notes with the tip of the bar and with no slides.

Going Down the Road Feeling Bad

"Going Down the Road," re-christened "Lonesome Road Blues" by Earl Scruggs, starts close to the melody, but by the end of the 3rd measure I bored myself, so a series of modular licks follows. Plug them into any one of hundreds of breakdowns with undeveloped themes (i.e., banjo tunes). Find the unadorned melody on your Dobro before learning the variations.

Hammering on and pulling off are not notated, but there are numerous obvious opportunities. In addition, the "melodic-style" part of measure 3 can be arranged for hammering and pulling.

Harvest Home Hornpipe

I play this Scottish hornpipe closer to the traditional rhythm than "Rickett's Hornpipe," but there is some ♪♪ character. Do not confuse the time-duration dots with the staccato-symbol dots.

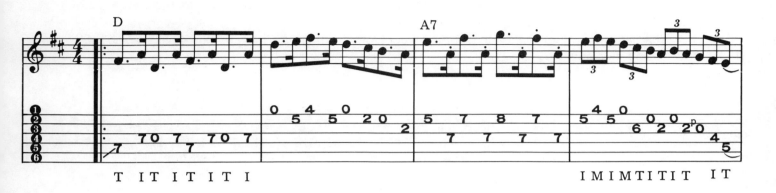

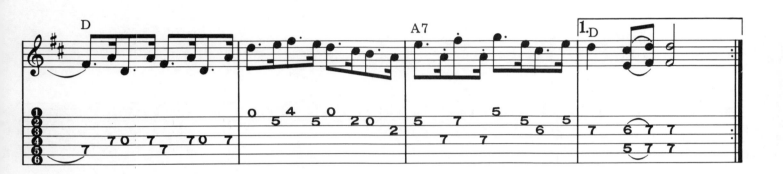

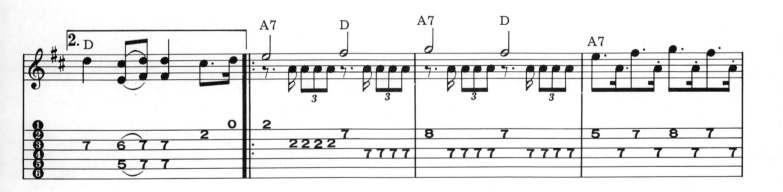

Home Sweet Home

This old nugget entered the world of Dobrodom through the playing of Buck Graves, the wondrous innovator of bluegrass Dobro. There are liberal amounts of him sprinkled through this version, especially in the first 8 measures.

Do not be frightened of the counter motion of the last 3 measures. It goes through a bit of unexpected dissonance before homing in on the final C chord.

Jennie Lind's rendition made "Home Sweet Home" America's number one smash hit of 1850. More about her presently.

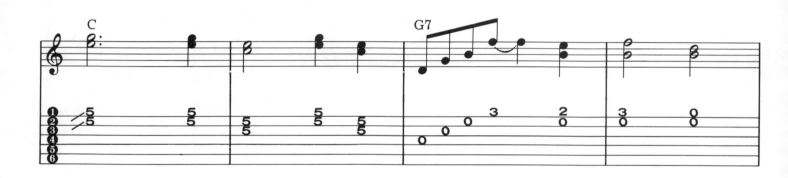

Tableau Clog Dance

I learned "Tableau Clog Dance" from Cecil Brower of the Light Crust Doughboys, a pioneer Western-swing band. There are some demanding bar manipulations here but, fortunately, "Tableau" is played at a brisk walking pace.

Note the key change in the middle. To end the tune, play the first section once.

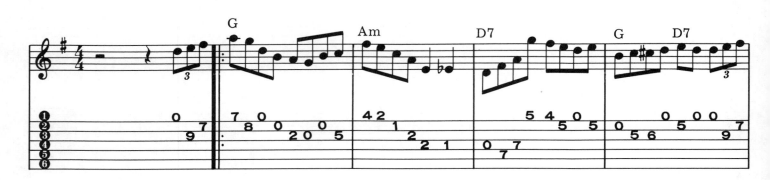

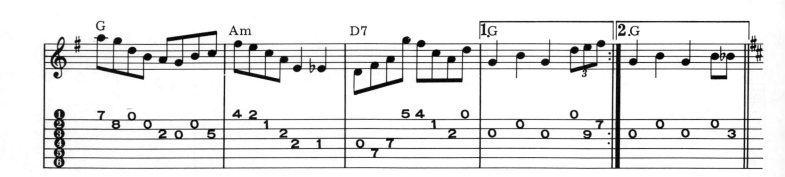

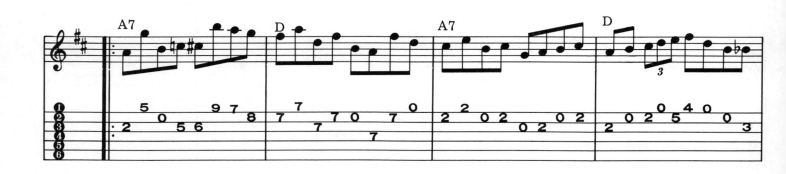

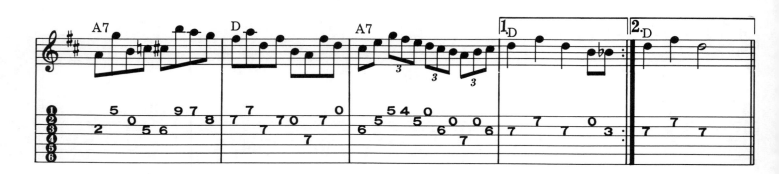

Buck Graves in the days of one microphone. When he stood on his toes and pivoted his Dobro towards the high mike, aficionados quivered with delight. Flatt and Scruggs share center stage with him here. (Photo courtesy of Artie Rose.)

The Irish Washerwoman

When the Irish first joined the "huddled masses, yearning to breathe free," they were subject to often violent rejection by earlier immigrants to America. Such work as taking in washing was the best that could be obtained. Dobro players who are in the job market can understand their plight.

I learned the joys of playing "Irish Washerwoman" in the key of A from that peerless pedagogue of the mandolin, Jack Tottle.

No slides, please.

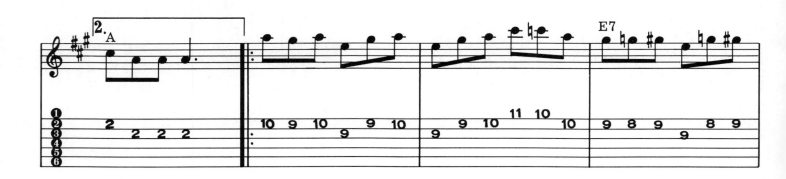

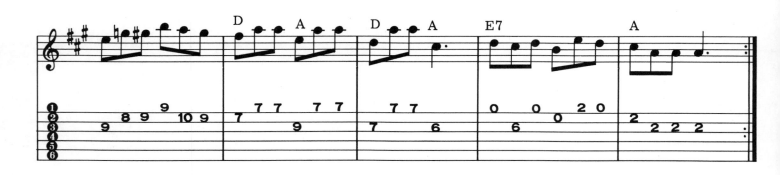

Poor Wayfaring Man of Grief

A pretty and melancholy, but slightly lugubrious waltz, "Wayfaring Man" is another tune I learned from the Deseret String Band.

Muddy Roads

"Muddy Roads" is from the playing of Gaither Carlton, an old-time fiddler from North Carolina. No doubt it will one day have words put to it and will become a country-Western hit.

The first section is arranged in banjo-ish fashion with droning G notes. Watch for the key change in the middle.

Play it over and over, medium fast and bouncy, until alpha-wave levels rise asymptotically.

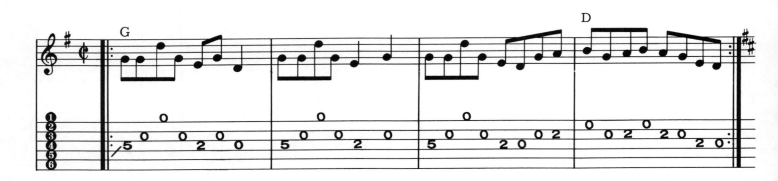

Wild Horse

"Wild Horse" is possibly the most named fiddle tune of historical times. Its aliases include "Stoney Point," "Warm Stuff," and "Pigtown Fling" — no kidding! The third section is not as widespread as the other two. This has much the same feel as "Muddy Roads."

Red Haired Boy

Capos ahoy! "Red Haired Boy" may have been introduced into bluegrass consciousness by Lonnie Pearce of those incipient newgrassers, The Bluegrass Alliance.

Please do not play this as a breakdown. A loping tempo is sufficient, thank you.

Capo on second fret

Arkansas Traveller

Here is a straightforward version of the constant-sixteenth-note school of fiddle tunes. (In cut-time meter these are notated as eighth notes.) Getting up to travelling speed is a finger-busting experience. In the 3rd measure, watch the legato symbols and keep the bar flat. The last four notes demand a slant position.

Southern Henny Youngman-types used to embroider this tune with the most outrageous country-rube-versus-city-slicker routines, starting with:

Slicker: Where does this road go?

Rube: It don't go nowhere, it stays right here all the time.

And culminating with:

Slicker: You don't seem to know too much of anything, do you?

Rube: Well, at least I ain't lost.

The most memorable performance of "Arkansas Traveller" was by the Bluegrass 45, who did the skits in their native Japanese. It was indescribable.

71

Martha Campbell

"Martha Campbell" is a Doc Roberts tune that demands some fast bar maneuvering. The first section is similar to "Ragtime Annie" but is usually played a little faster. Try to play the first 3 measures without slides. An easy alternate to the 15th measure is given for the faint of heart.

Alternate 15th measure

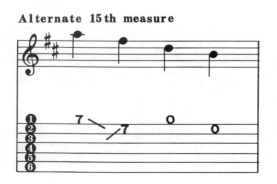

Fire on the Mountain

Fiddlers usually play "Fire on the Mountain" as fast as possible. It changes keys and has the old-timey touch of an additional 2 measures at the end of each go-around to get back to the key of A.

The first section is fretted in pseudo-melodic banjo style. The 1st measure is a run that will appear with hammer-ons and pull-offs elsewhere in the book. Keep an ear out.

Capo on second fret

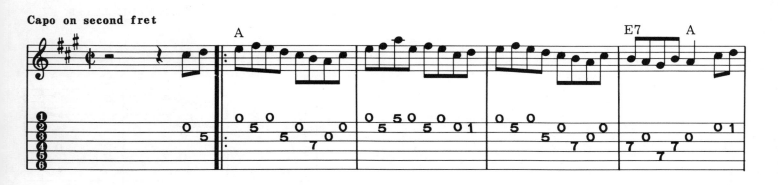

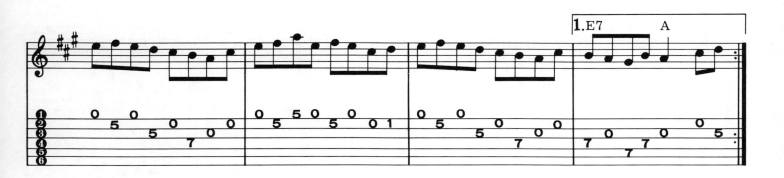

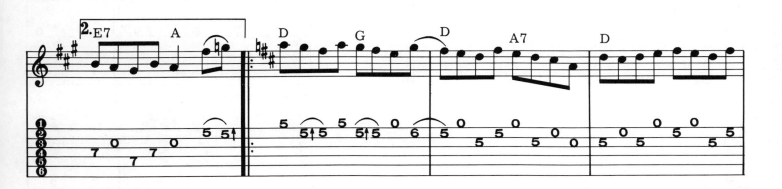

Si Bheag Si Mhor

A poignant waltz that translates from Gaelic as "So Big, So Little." Play this one slowly, with pathos and a bit of bathos.

The first section is arranged to allow for overlapping notes, so obey the tie lines. In measures 9, 10, 13, and 14, the treble staff is divided in two, to indicate that one set of notes sustains while the others are picked.

At the beginning of the 19th measure, there is a quick thumb scrape in which all the strings except the first are muted.

Peekaboo Waltz

I learned "Peekaboo Waltz" from the playing of Pappy Sherrill. It is a sure-fire hit at your next ice-skating party. Play it on the fast side as far as waltzes go. Not the funkiest of tunes, but nice to hear and pretty easy to play.

Remember, the legato sign means slide from the indicated note and pick the next one.

Fisher's Hornpipe

I used to play "Fisher's Hornpipe" in G or else capoed up 7 frets to play in D (with G fretting). In this book, all D tunes are done without a capo, and no deviationism will be allowed to achieve hegemony over this concept.

You should pick the notes loudly, because continuous low notes on the Dobro tend to get muddied by the sustain of the open strings. (No one said that there would be no complications.)

Hornpipes were originally played on reeded animal horns before fiddles got a hold of them. So much for the sanctity of fiddle tunes.

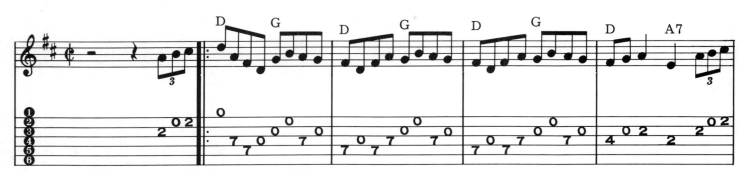

MITIMITI

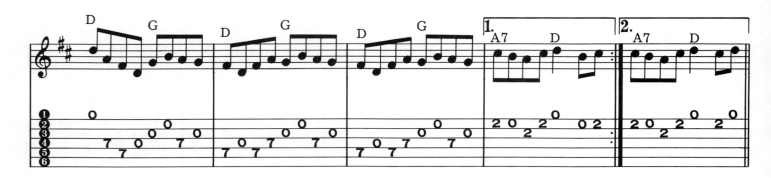

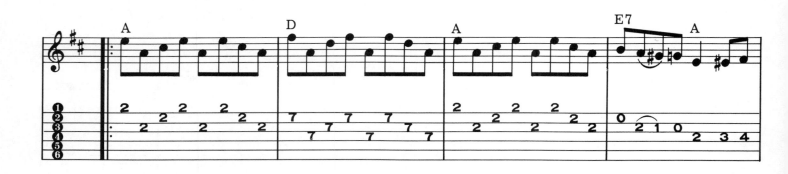

Nine Miles Out of Louisville

"Nine Miles Out of Louisville" is from the playing of Kentuckian Buddy Thomas. In the 5th measure, I elected to pick each note separately. Inserting a judicious slide might make it a bit easier.

Working this tune out made me perspire. If you have been going along in the book, you should be getting used to riffs like the ones in measures 3 through 6. In the keys of G, C, and D, they pop up regularly.

Alternate fifth measure

Pal of Mine

This is another traditional tune that Buck Graves introduced to Mondo Dobro when he was a Foggy Mountain Boy with Lester Flatt and Earl Scruggs, but there is less of him in this arrangement than in "Home Sweet Home." I have tried to keep the melody within hailing distance at all times as it bobs and weaves across the ledger lines.

In the 12th measure, there is a downward scrape with the index finger to ease accenting of the E note.

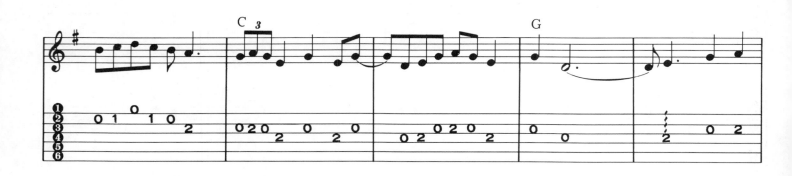

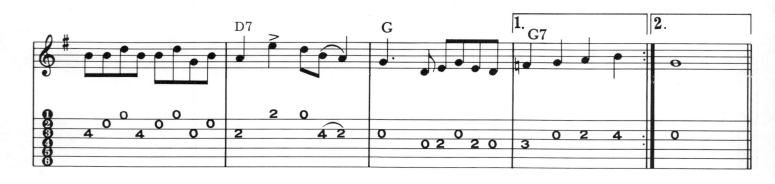

Cripple Creek

Here is a nice old tune that has been wrestled to submission by scores of unfeeling musicians. You can practice it as you listen to the *Hee Haw* television show.

A particularly aimless tag is appended for your sneering and fleering pleasure.

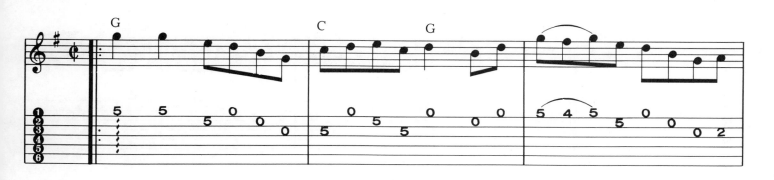

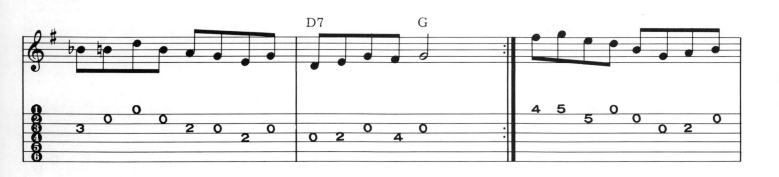

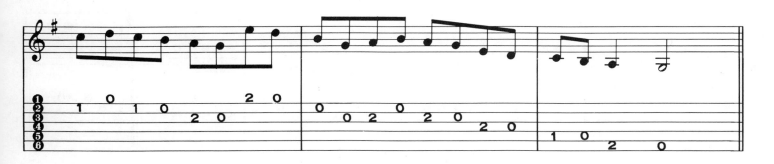

Texas Gales

I learned this euphoric number from the band that came on with the power of gale-force winds, the late, lamented Wretched Refuse String Band. If nothing else, it is a good exercise for the key of C. Set your metronome just short of "real fast."

The Northwest Chapter of the Order of the Resophonicists perform at the Puget Sound Guitar Workshop. Seventeen sliders scintillated on "Little Green Pill." The musical director directs traffic. (Photo by Larry Squire.)

Jennie Lind

This old timer is named for the Swedish Nightingale, Johanna "Jennie" Lind (1820–1887), probably the first intercontinental superstar. The greatest opera diva of her time, she had a vocal range from B below the staff line to G above high C. Wow! She inspired several of Hans Christian Anderson's stories, including "The Ugly Duckling." (He was sweet on her and did not trust his looks.)

P. T. Barnum, of all people, arranged a tour of America that blew the socks off the whole country. Among the offshoots of Lindomania were compositions like "Jennie Lind Polka," "Jennie Lind Waltz," and the "Jennie Lind Galop." This piece found its way into the fade-out of Bill Monroe's classic autobiographical song, "Uncle Pen." He did it in the key of A.

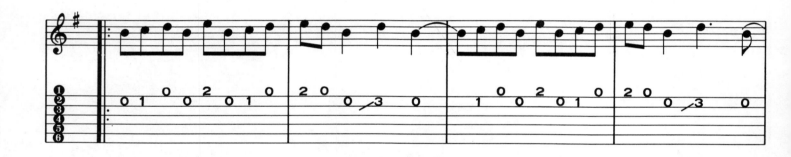

The Swedish Nightingale.

Three Sea Captains

I got this jig out of a book of fiddle tunes years ago, and I have yet to hear it played. Here is my guess as to how it sounds with a possible chord progression.

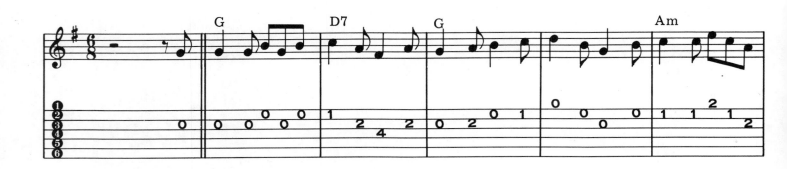

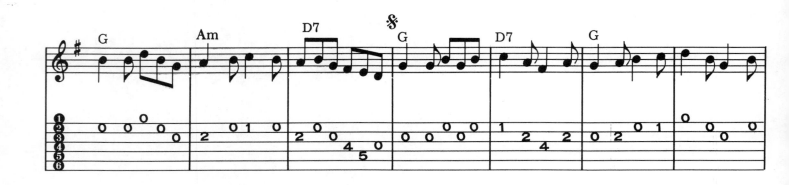

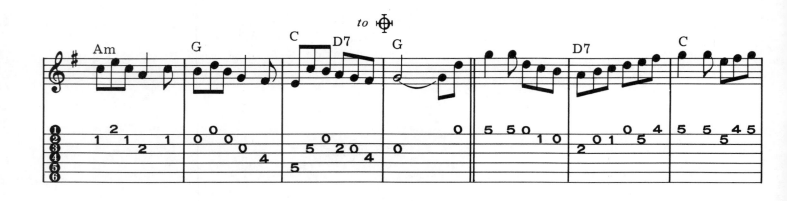

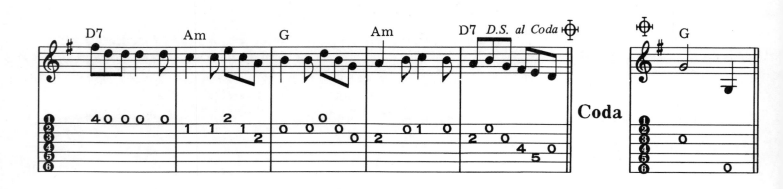

The Rover Reformed

I learned the slow, English "The Rover Reformed" from Robin Williamson's fine book of British fiddle tunes. Its melodic minor scale paints a somber mood that works well against the usually jaunty jig rhythm and is especially effective with a Dobro's tone.

The second section is a rare bird among the fiddle tunes I know, in that it has a 16-measure melody as opposed to the usual 8-bar type that might be repeated with variations. The chord progression is striking, too. The trill on the last A7 chord can be thought of as an overwrought vibrato between the 2nd and 3rd frets.

Has the rover reformed from his rambling ways, or has he re-formed his old life-style after quitting his job at IBM?

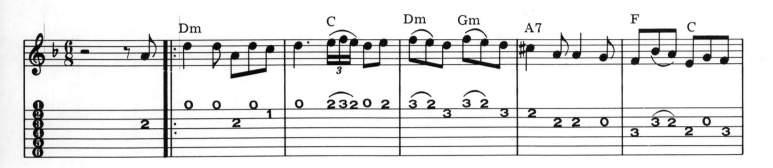

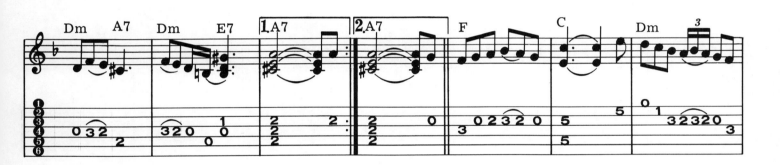

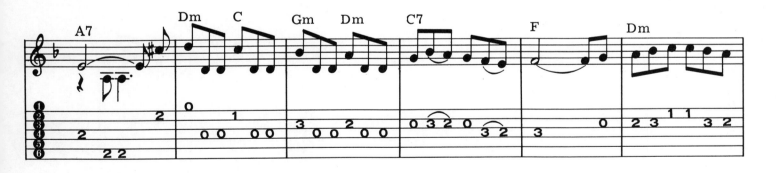

Lead Out

The happy "Lead Out" is adapted from the playing of Tommy Jackson, one of the creators of the standard commercial-country fiddle style. This tune is also known as "Chinky Pin" and "Too Young to Marry."

In the 2nd measure of the second section, start a slow slide down right after you pick the fourth string, 7th fret, then do a quick slide up to the fifth string, 7th fret.

As in several previous tunes, I have fretted the F♯-G-F♯ series of notes alternately as a choke (2nd measure), or a slide, or picked separately (3rd measure). It is a combination of which sounds best, is easier, or feels right when I tape it. Check the alternative 1st and 2nd measures for other examples.

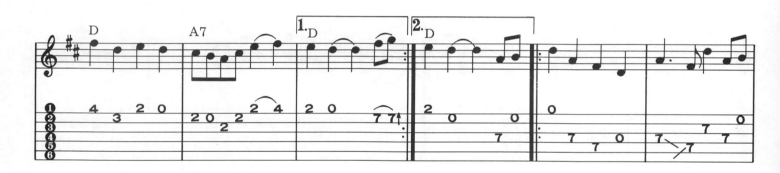

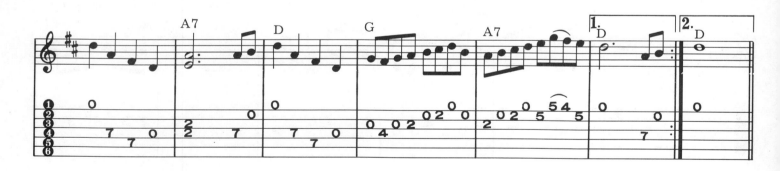

Alternate tenth measure

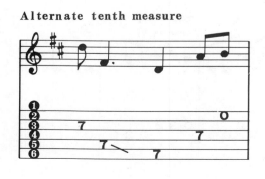

Alternate 1st & 2nd measures

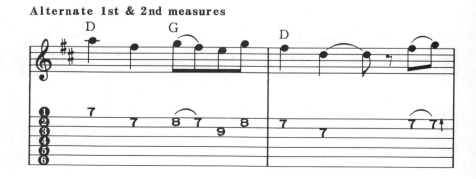

Drowsy Maggie

Back to the British Isles with "Drowsy Maggie," an evergreen Irish reel. At the fast tempos at which this is sometimes played, the triplets are voluntary.

It feels like this tune is in E minor, but it uses a D major scale. To end it, you might slow down in the last measure and then strum an E minor.

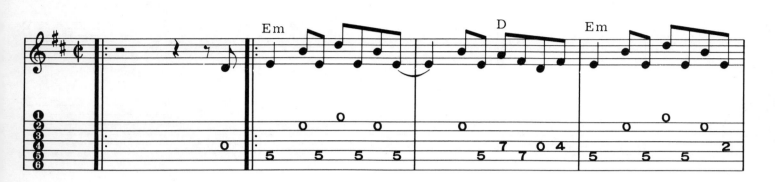

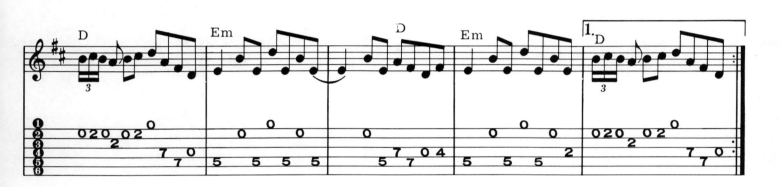

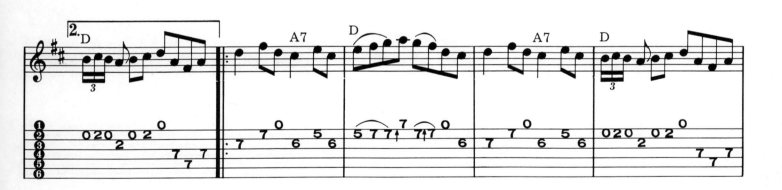

The Bishop of Bangor

"The Bishop of Bangor" is a Welsh jig with a nice chord progression. It is another one that I have never heard, but I like the way it sounds on tape. The second part is full of tricky but handy licks. *Bangor* means "church with a woven fence" in Welsh.

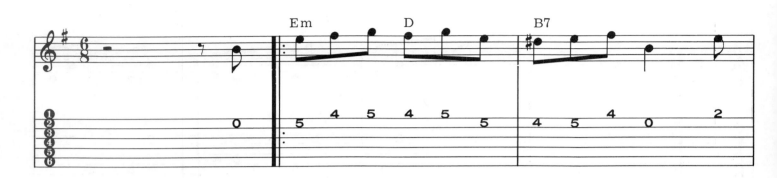

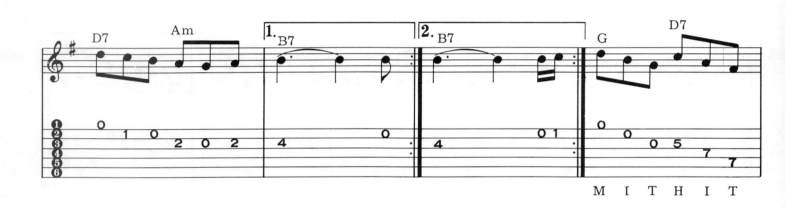

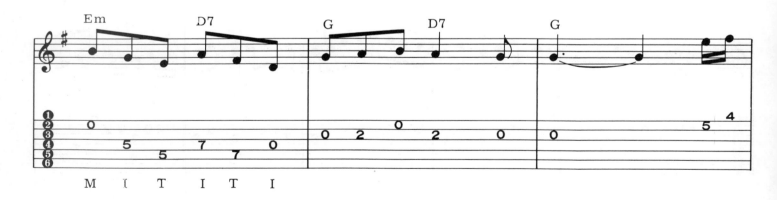

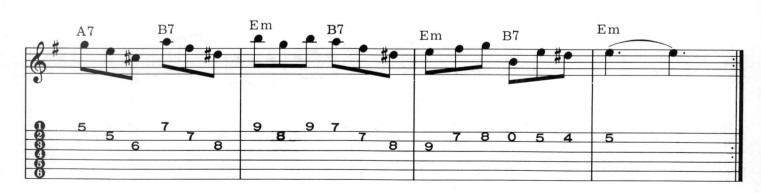

Peter Gray

And now an up-tempo reel from the mammoth repertoire of the peerless Scottish fiddler, James Scott Skinner, the winner of the big Inverness Jamboree and Violin Competition in 1863. His tunes are often showcases for his high-powered technique, and "Peter Gray" is a suitable challenge for Dobroists. Your fingers have to skip strings a lot, and this jumping around can be tough at high speed. All in all, it is a challenging and rewarding piece of music.

On the back of one of his compositions Skinner wrote, "Simplicity of form does not necessarily mean dearth of genius." So do not let any jazz or classical jokers put down your breakdowns.

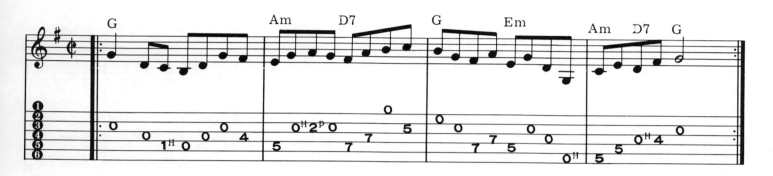

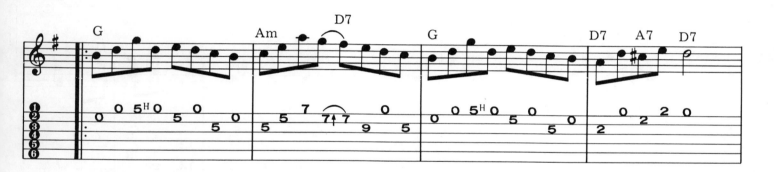

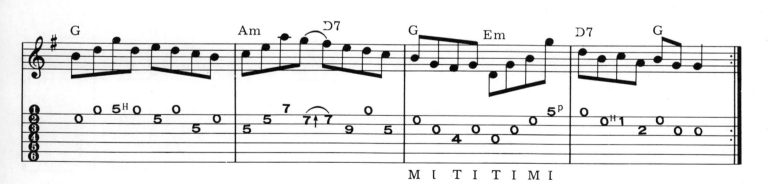

M I T I T I M I

Alternate 2nd measure

89

Cuckoo's Nest
(British Version)

The dainty air "Cuckoo's Nest" completes this mini-array of British tunes. This one is from the arsenal of David Swarbrick. It is easy and it sounds nice. Relax. Once again, you have the choice of playing the notes marked as ⅄‧⅄ somewhere between ⅄‧⅄ and ⅄⅄‧⅄ . I play it close to the latter.

The alternate 11th and 14th measures give ideas for other fretting possibilities. Variations of slides and non-slides, and fretting mutations are endless, especially on slow tunes. Fooling around with them can lead to subtle but suggestive discoveries.

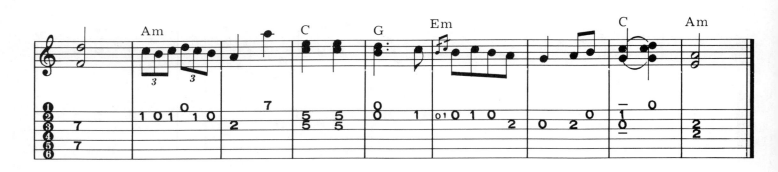

Alternate 11th measure

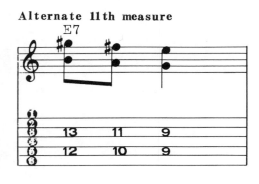

Alternate 14th measure

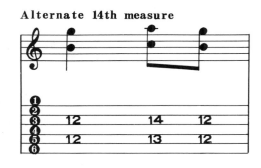

Corridor on a Danish ferry (photo by Eric Levenson).

When You and I Were Young, Maggie

And now a gracious acknowledgment of the prodigal grandson of the Hawaiian guitar, the ubiquitous pedal steel. The pedals change the pitch of a string without having to move the bar, and a similar effect can be achieved by choking with your ring or middle finger. The quintessential pedal-steel lick brings the pitch of the second note of the scale up to that of the third (in the key of G, an A note raised to a B). By tuning the second string down to an A and then choking 2 frets' worth, a similar sound can be achieved on the old hound-dog guitar.

I think this "ninth" tuning (for technical reasons, the second note of a scale is often referred to by its identity one octave higher, the ninth note of a scale) has lots of possibilities besides the chordal ideas exposed here. I have used it on cuts on albums by Tony Trischka, Tasty Licks and Hazel Dickens and Alice Foster. Shot Jackson once built an acoustic pedal resonator guitar and recorded something like this with Buddy Emmons. (He called it "Hound Dog Blues.")

At the end of the 7th measure of the second section, start a slow slide up to the 14th fret as soon as you pick the fourth string, 12th fret. There are half, single, and 2-fret chokes used here, so pay attention to the traffic signals.

There are some quite groovy single-string licks that are easy in any key that have an A note in the scale. To exhibit some tricks you can do with choking, I have put in examples at almost every possible point. If you overdo an effect like this, it can lose its charm fast. Ordinarily I would probably cut down on this gimmick if someone were listening.

92

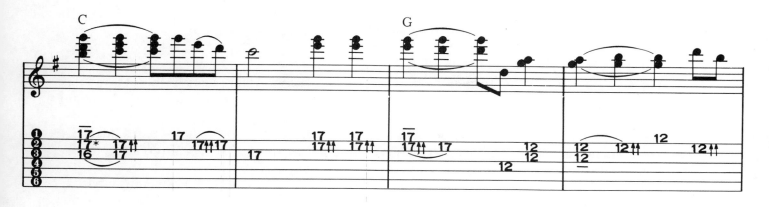

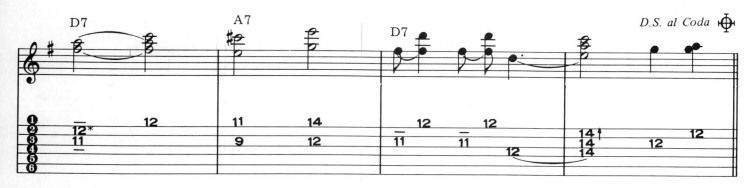

D.S. al Coda

Coda

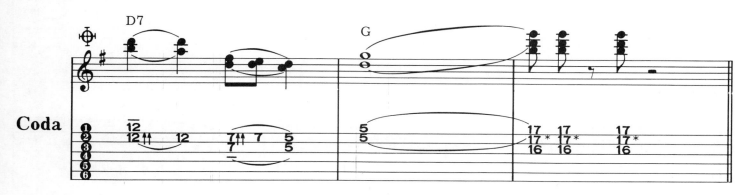

Alternate 2nd measure of first ending (1st section)

Alternate 6th measure of second section

Leather Britches

I have heard that "Leather Britches" refers to a part of the cotton plant that resembles trousers. Having been raised in New York City, I would not know a cotton plant if it mugged me. Leather britches have quite a different connotation for a native of that congenial sink of depravity.

This is one of the tunes that collects a myriad of variations, supplied by contest-crazed fiddlers. I taped one version and added another first section in the book to give you the idea. In contests, tunes are played at medium tempos to highlight clarity and smoothness of playing.

The second section of "Leather Britches" has always been kind of nebulous. This setting is based on the playing of one of the kingpins of the Texas contest style, Benny Thomasson. It calls for similar barring maneuvers as "Lead Out."

A 2-measure tag is appended. On the tape the tag runs on like bad gasoline and becomes whimsical.

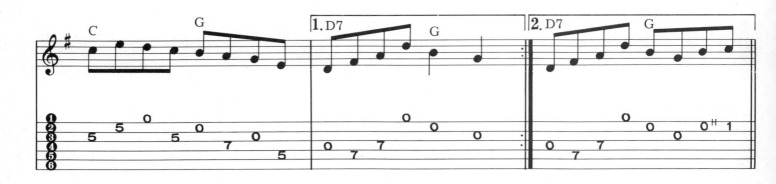

94

Ragtime Annie

The opening measures of "Ragtime Annie" are tough to play cleanly at its usual bouncy tempo. Try them without any slides.

You can use just the index finger and thumb, alternately, to pick the 5th and 6th measures of the second section instead of the indicated pattern. In the same measures, you could also slide the F♯-G-F♯ lick instead of picking each note separately (as in the 3rd measure of section three).

End with either section one or two.

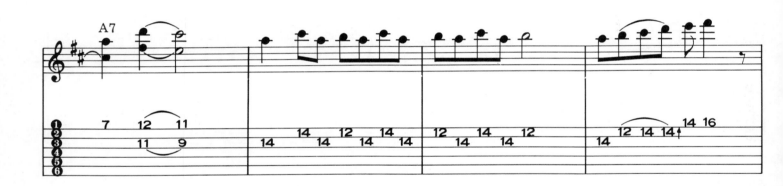

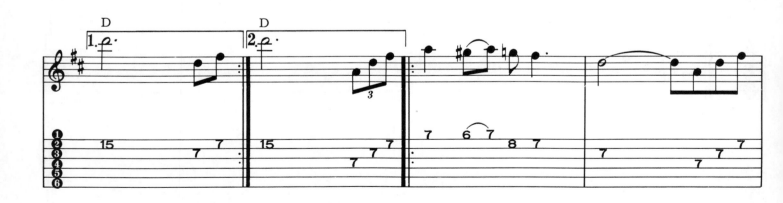

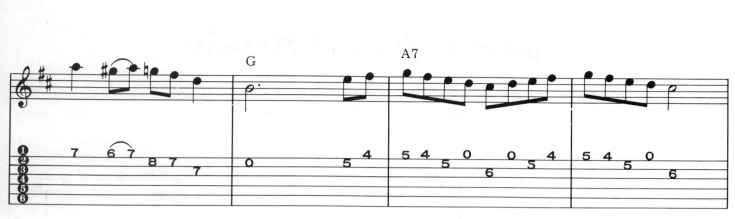

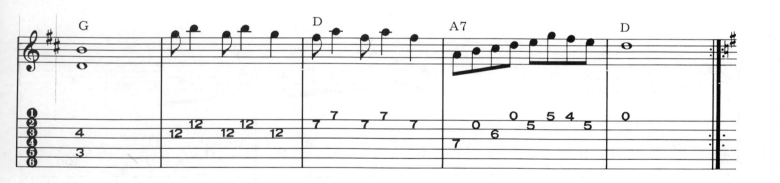

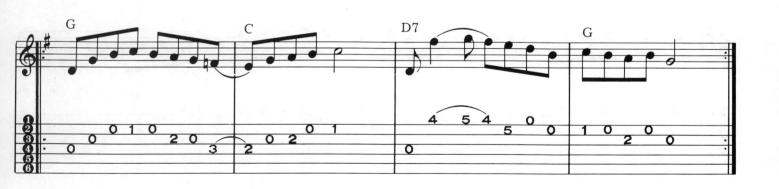

Black Eyed Susie

This version of "Black Eyed Susie" is based on the ancient recording of Doc Roberts and should be played at a danceable tempo. Nothing fancy, but it is a nice version of the melody.

Katy Hill

    A popular tune with fiddlers, "Katy Hill" is noteworthy for its shadowy melody. The second section is especially obscure. It is usually played extra fast.

    An alternate 1st measure (which also serves as measures 3 and 5) and measures 14 and 15 have been added. The latter two are heisted from Kenny Baker's version.

99

The Hen's March to the Midden

It is time for a Stacy Phillips "salute to chickens." One of the all-time favorites for old-time tune titles, chicken-like sound effects follow only steam-driven trains and diesel horns in popularity. Over the years clucks, bucks, and squawks have pealed throughout the corridors of fiddle music and have been adapted by other instruments.

The first selection in my praise-the-pullet section is a Shetland Island tune that translates as "The Hen's March to the Garbage Heap." They are marching and not scurrying, so do not play it fast.

Watch out for the tricky timing in the 7th measure. The clucks start in the second section. The notes in parentheses are held as short as possible and can be dampened as indicated or played very staccato. The double accent marks indicate especially strong stress. The G#° chord is strictly voluntary.

In the alternate version of part two, the 1st through 4th measures, the damped and sounded notes are reversed. Mix and match both versions.

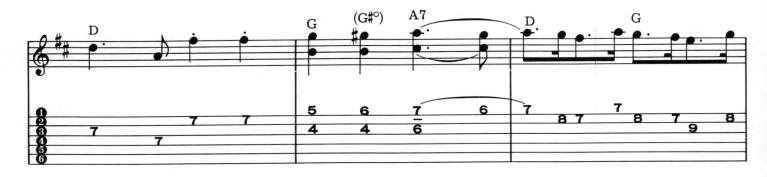

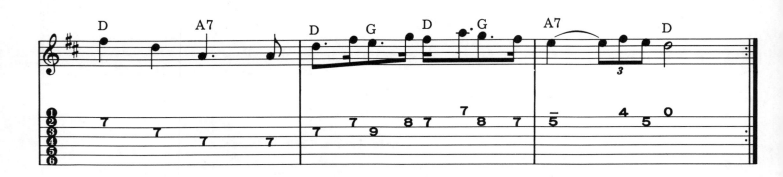

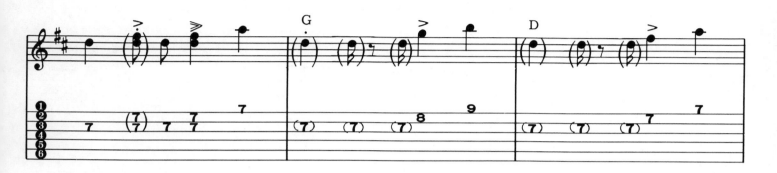

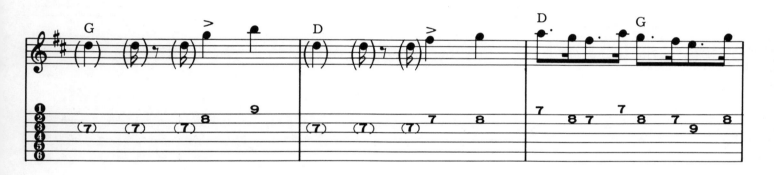

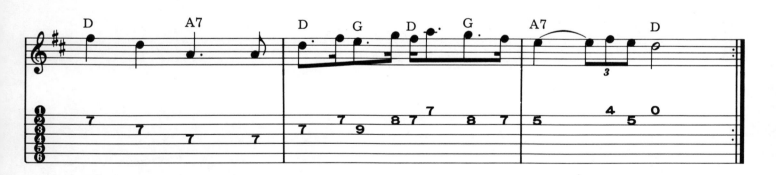

Alternate 9th & 10th measures

Cackling Hen

More strange scratches and burps, as in "The Hen's March," the staid first section suddenly erupts into barnyard cackles.

In the third section the slide to the first string, 2nd fret, should be quick, rewarding us with a squawking noise.

> "My old hen, she's mighty kind,
> Every time she cackles, an egg you'll find.
> The old hen cackled, she cackled in the lot,
> Next time she cackled, she cackled in the pot."

Let us honor her ultimate sacrifice with the music of her species.

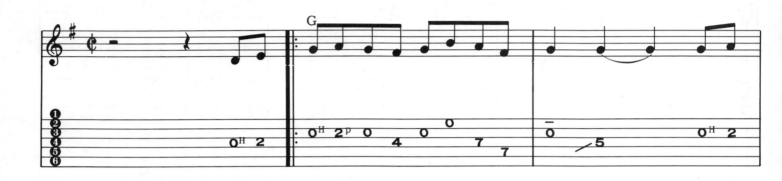

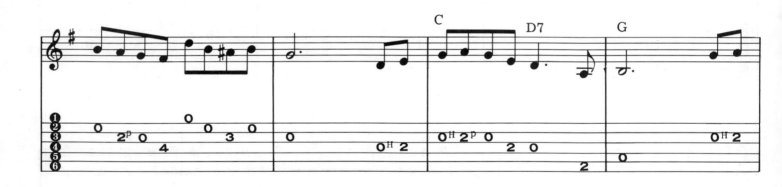

I T I T

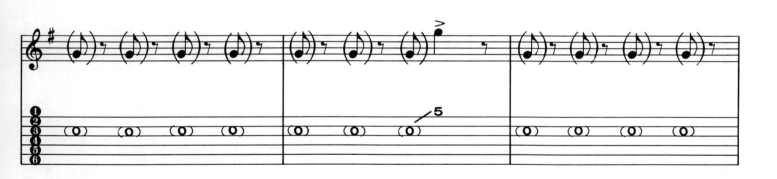

103

Chicken Reel

Now it is time for some swinging, trucking cluckers. Play "Chicken Reel" with plenty of bounce, almost as a swing tune (i.e., play each pair of eighth notes as tied triplets, ♪♪♪).

Try playing the entire first section of the second version with your thumb and index finger. There are quite a few crossovers (index playing a lower string than the thumb, or the thumb a higher one than the index). Once you overcome these problems, using these two fingers (almost as a flatpick) can be simpler than worrying about a third finger. Then you need use only three fingers when doing Scruggs-type rolls. Of course, this section works with hammer-ons and pull-offs and three fingers if you wish to be bourgeois.

Cluck Old Hen

Let us bid farewell to these fowl most fair with some ominous, power-chording, angry hens. Part of this old timer was turned into a rock riff in the '60s, and it echoes in the optional chord progression and the alternate measures that follow the main body of the tune.

Play it at a trot with a foreboding blues feel. The mixolydian G scale has an F♮ instead of the usual F♯.

"Cluck old hen, cluck and sing,
Ain't laid an egg since way last spring.
Cluck old hen, cluck and squall,
One day chickens gonna rule the world."

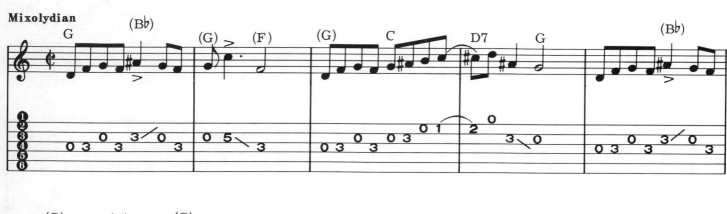

Alternate third and fourth measures

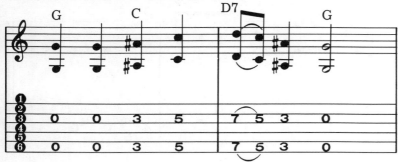

Jaybird

Jaybirds have the reputation of being loud and foolish, but this version I learned from Kenny Kosek is a pretty old-timey tune made for a danceable tempo.

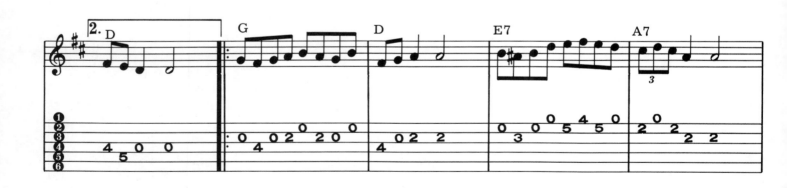

Southfork Bluegrass Band of Bellingham, Wash., at a typical "picking" session. Left to right - Standing: Peter Schwimmer, Cliff Perry, "Grady" Brackett. Seated: Stacy Phillips, Jack Hansen.

(Photo by Holly Henderson.)

Photo by Dave Howard.

Ebba Polka

Polkas can be Dobro tunes, too. "Ebba Polka" is from an old recording by the Ukrainian band Trembita Orchestra. One polka strategy to keep musicians' interest during extended dance sessions is to modulate at each new section. Here we have C, G, and F represented.

Do the first section once in between the second and third. The third section contains a most wonderful bar position in measures 5 and 6. Use a reverse slant, and let the notes overlap. I have mercifully allowed a quarter-note rest beforehand to let you arrange the bar.

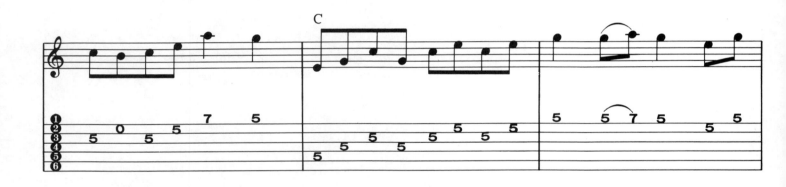

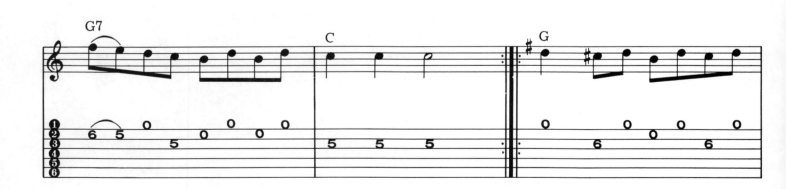

Bull Hill Hornpipe

Like Ukrainian polkas, typical American hornpipe ploys are modulations to related keys. In my personal contribution to the genre, there are two such changes. The order of playing is: part one with repeat, part two with repeat, part one once, and part three. To end the tune, play the first part one more time and substitute the alternate 6th measure with a B7 chord instead of a B minor.

The first two sections may sound nice with a swing-type rhythm section, then switch to an old-timey or bluegrass backup for the third part.

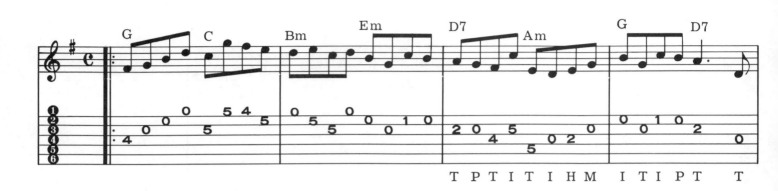

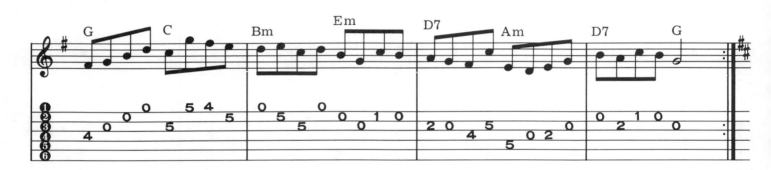

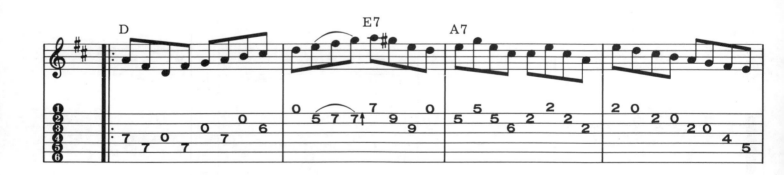

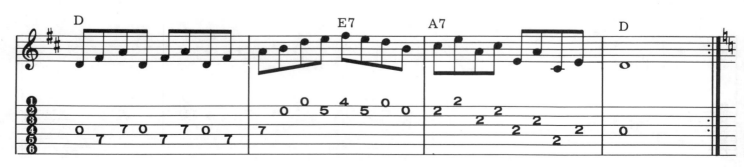

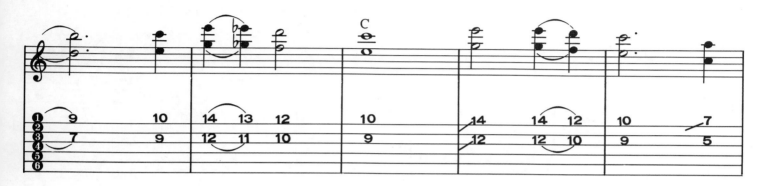

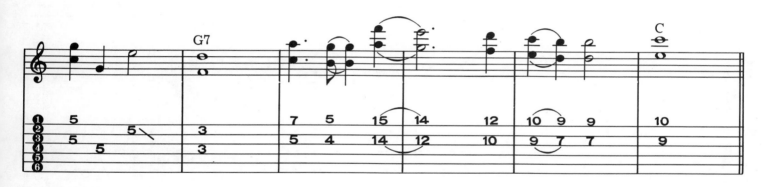

Alternate 10th measure

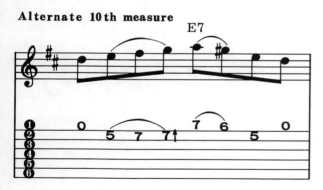

Alternate 6th measure—Last time only

Cuckoo's Nest
(Texas Version)

This must be related somehow to the British version, though this is faster and modal instead of minor. Both David Swarbrick and Texas Shorty Chancellor play their versions with a light bow. We can do the same by not picking as hard as on most of the up-tempo tunes in this book.

The challenge here is playing arpeggios up and down all six strings. If you have six fingers and picks, it is pretty easy. Otherwise, your right hand has to move around to get to all the strings consecutively. Try using your thumb for part of the arpeggio, as in the 3rd measure. I use three different fingerings for these similar licks to demonstrate the possibilities, and as a personal exercise. Compare the fingering and fretting for the related licks in measures 5, 6, 13, and 14.

Jerry Douglas observes the audience (photo by Eric Levenson).

Salt River

And now a special treat for all who have persevered through all the previous tunes. "Salt River" is a traditional fiddle tune I learned from Clark Kessinger.

The first version is in A without a capo and set in the spirit of the old-time style. Its modal flavor (sort of half major and half minor) makes it easy to play without a "cheater."

The second version is arranged in a modern bluegrass setting. I have taken pains to present it in the style of the day's most popular Dobroist, Mr. Jerry "Flux" Douglas. The origin of his nickname is shrouded in mystery, but scuttlebutt has its etymology connected with bodily functions.

There is a 2-measure introduction to the first arrangement. Play the opening three-string slide with wild abandon. The capoed version exhibits Douglas' fine sense of syncopation (check out the last 7 measures) mixed with unrelenting flurries of fast runs.

114

Capo on second fret ("Jerry Douglas Style")

Staten Island Hornpipe

A standard British-type hornpipe. Could "Staten Island" have been written for the New York City borough? Is there another Staten Island somewhere?

The first 2 measures of the second section are similar to the same part of "Arkansas Traveller," so similar licks can be used. In the two alternatives to these measures, I have mixed parts of both tunes. At the end of each, you can slide from the 2nd fret to the 5th and continue.

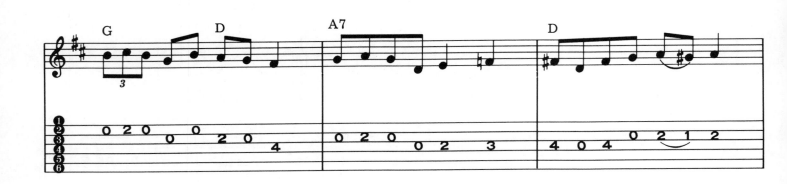

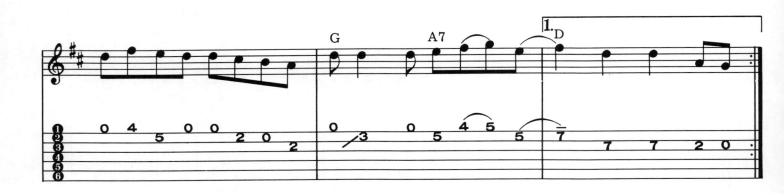

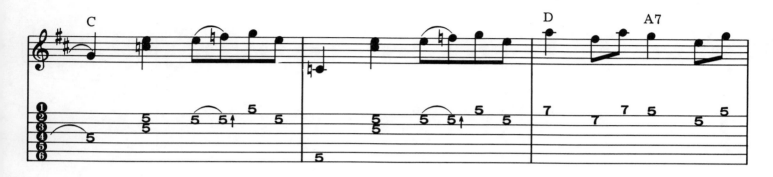

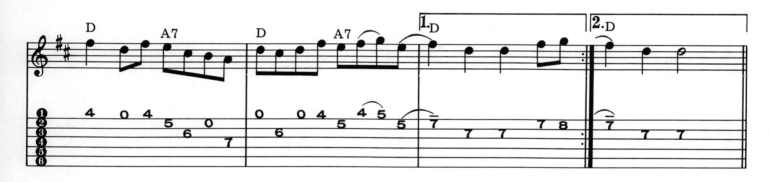

Alternate 9th & 10th measures

Additional Alternate 9th & 10th measures

Rose of Sharon

I learned "Rose of Sharon" from another Mel Bay book, *Deluxe Fiddling Method* by Craig Duncan. A rose of Sharon is mentioned in the biblical "Song of Solomon" and is the name of Tom Joad's sister in *The Grapes of Wrath*.

The 7th measure ab-uses what the trade calls a suspended fourth (here an A note in an E chord). Measures 23 and 24 contain a hellacious contrary-motion lick never before attempted on a six-string steel. The 14th measure has a pedal-point-type lick, with an easier alternative given at the end of the tablature.

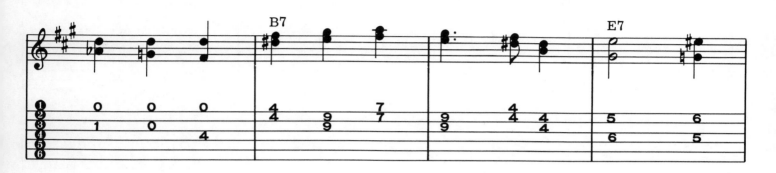

Alternate measure 14 & 30

My Little Home in West Virginia

This version of "My Little Home in West Virginia" is based on the stylings of the Chairman of Bluegrass Dobro, Burkett "Uncle Josh" Graves. I have tried to decipher the fretting he uses, an important part of his sound. The short bluesy run in the 7th measure of the second section is another of Graves' trademarks, especially when it comes in the midst of a non-blues tune.

Josh Graves (photo by Jim McGuire).

Down Yonder

I let myself go a bit on this standard breakdown, so there are many syncopations and bursts of random G-scale patterns. Occasionally the melody passes out of radar range, so keep on your toes. Personally, I think this is a pretty good rendition, sure to wow them at the next picking session.

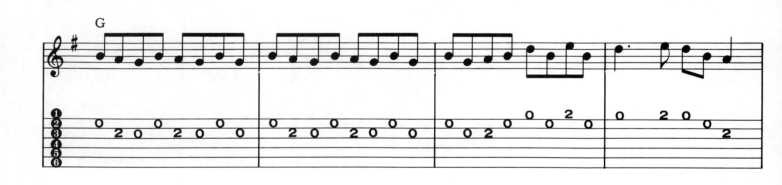

123

Outwood Echoes

Outwood is a perky village in Surrey, England, where I was gloriously patronized by the gentry and Polydor Records during an extended visit. Anyone out there remember the Orange Blossom Sound?

I recorded this as part of my recovery therapy after two years of playing with the bad boys of bluegrass, Breakfast Special. It is on a deservedly obscure album, *All Old Friends* (on Revonah Records), which can be found at your local plumbing-supply outlet.

I am suspect of the pedigree of the scale young Stacy used, but it still can jangle the nerves a bit. Certainly there is no such key signature as this. Play this with a mildly calypso rhythm.

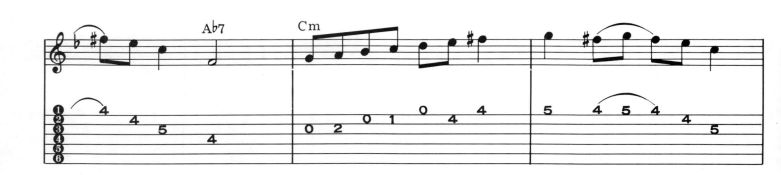

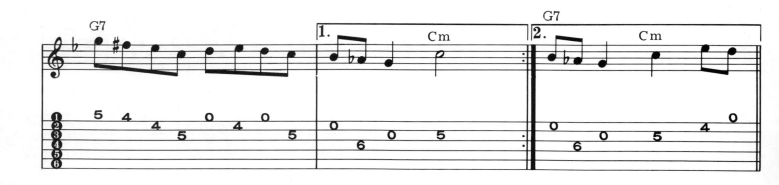

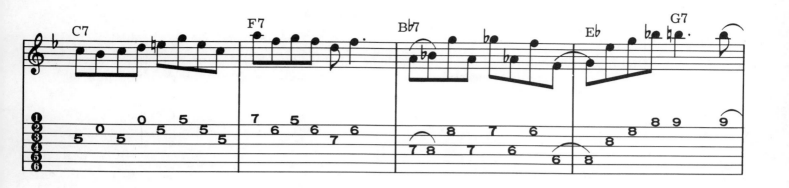

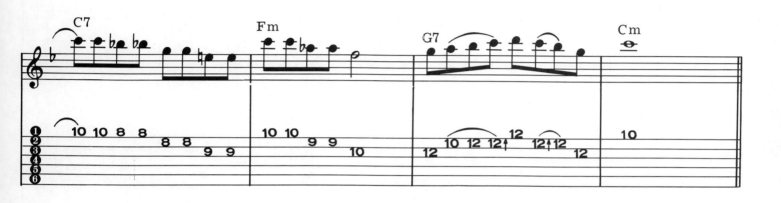

Alternate second section

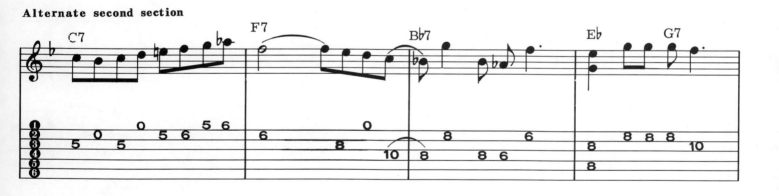

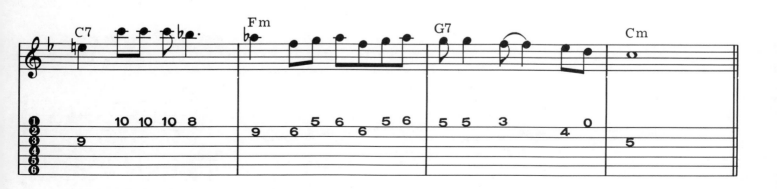

125

On Top

To mark this new edition of my Dobro tune books, I have included some blues tunes. These should offset the almost unbearable cheerfulness of the up-tempo material that makes up the bulk of this book.

Play this slowly with much vibrato.

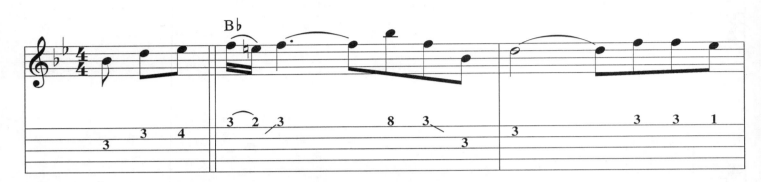

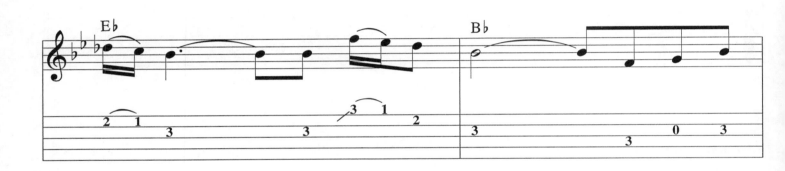

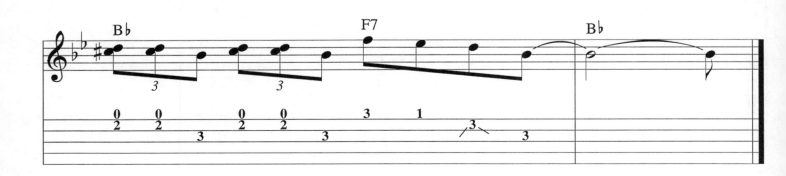

Dust My Broom

Play this Chicago-style boogie on the quick side and swing the eighth notes like crazy. the first few measures are made up of some clichéd bottleneck guitar licks. Try to vibrato while you play the triplet figures.

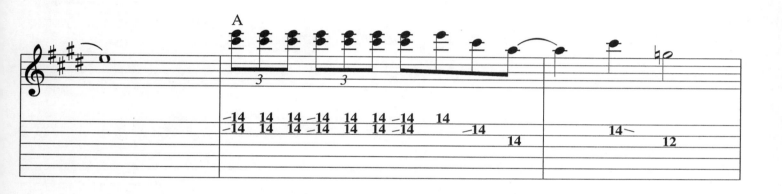

Country Blues

When bluegrass Dobroists play blues in the key of G, they inevitably wind up picking the open and 3rd frets, as in measures 1 through 5 of this arrangement. Play this number from slow to medium tempos.

The final measures contain a typical blues tag which often ritards to a final stop.

Trouble in Mind

I often play the 3rd measure in slant position. This allows the B note to continue sounding as the bar slides on the second string. It is perfectly acceptable for the slide to go a bit past the 8th fret in a blues setting. The controlled dissonance of playing "in the cracks" between frets can sound great in this context.

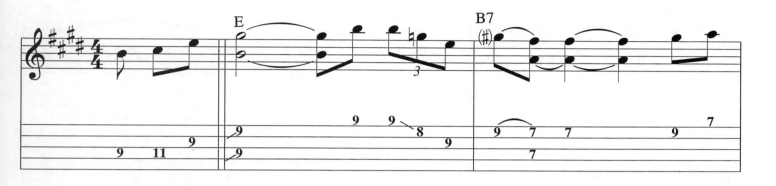

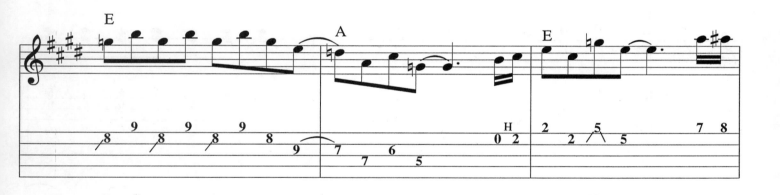

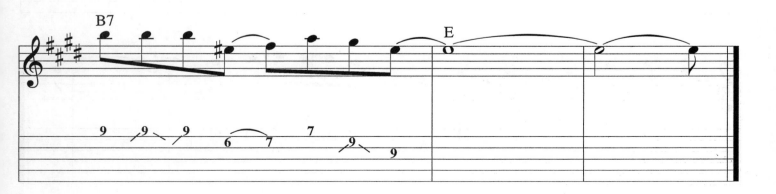

Country Boogie Number One

There is a relatively long kickoff to this score, so be careful to hit a bit of an accent on the first note after the double line (A♭). Swing those eighths!

Nice and Easy

The trick in this number is to leave the low G sounding on the open bottom string while playing the double stops that follow in the first 4 measures. This is accomplished by exerting some extra pressure on the second string, which tilts the bar a bit to allow it to lift off of the sixth string while still keeping it on the fourth string.

Measure 11 features my favorite Jimi Hendrix chord which he used so effectively on "Purple Haze." Why he did not use a Dobro is a mystery to me.

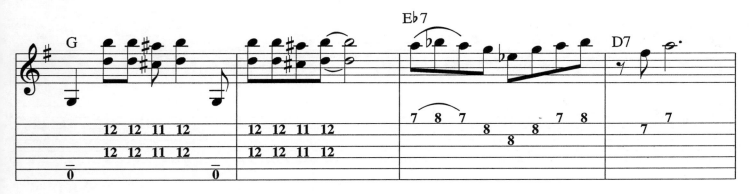

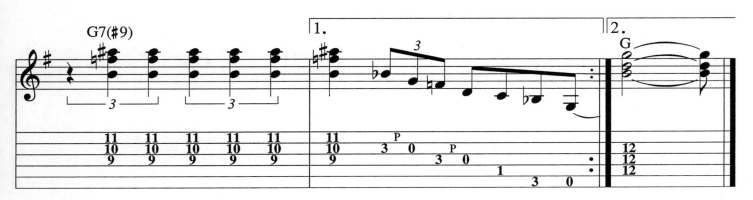

Country Boogie Number Two

Play this entirely with the tip of the bar. The last 2 measures are a typical blues tag.

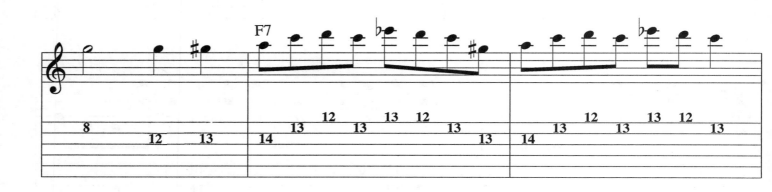

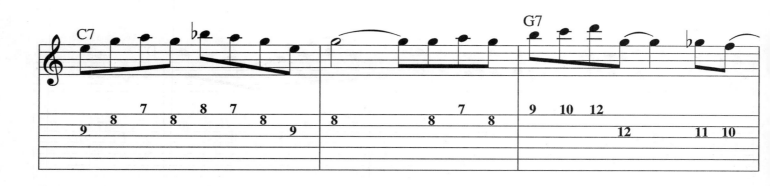

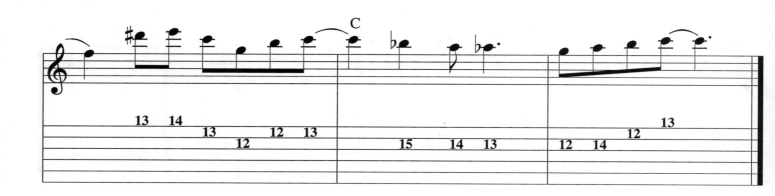

Bibliography

Here are some of my other Dobro publications in which you might be interested. All are available from me. I can be contacted through Mel Bay Publications, Inc., P.O. Box 66, Pacific, MO 63069-0066.

The Dobro Book: An overview of techniques and styles through the years.

Beginning Dobro: An introduction to the basic techniques.

The Dobro Chord Book: Effective chord positions for every type of chord you will ever meet, with examples of their use in tunes.

The Art of Hawaiian Steel Guitar: An in-depth look at the old style of acoustic Hawaiian guitar, with over 60 tablatures by Sol Hoopii, Benny Nawahi, Jim and Bob, etc.

The Complete Dobroist: An in-depth guide to all the musical styles a Dobro player should know — blues, country, ballads, bluegrass, and swing — with particular attention to the most influential Dobroists. Includes interviews, music theory for Dobro, and an overview on techniques. (Available in 1994.)

Bluegrass Dobro: A six-hour cassette course covering all aspects of bluegrass licks and solos, from the basics to the hottest licks.

Mike Auldridge, Jerry Douglas, and Stacy Phillips conducting a Dobro seminar (courtesy Thomas Flynn).